MW01290655

Getting High

The Annapurna Circuit in Nepal

by Bill Walker

Skywalker Publishing

Printer: createspace.com
ISBN-13 9781482598506
ISBN-10 1482598507

Dedication

The Annapurna Area Conservation Project (ACAP), one of the Himalaya's most successful environmental programs, for minimizing the damage to the Annapurna region.

Disclaimer

The book describes the author's experiences while walking the Annapurna Circuit and reflects his opinions relating to those experiences. Others may recall these same events differently. A couple names and identifying details mentioned in the book have been changed to protect their privacy.

Also by Bill Walker

Skywalker – Close Encounters on the Appalachian Trail (2008)

Skywalker – Highs and Lows on the Pacific Crest Trail (2010)

The Best Way – El Camino de Santiago (2012)

Map of Annapurna Circuit

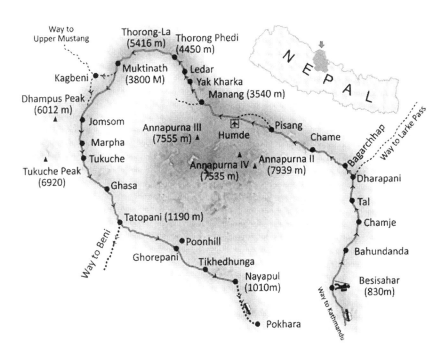

CHAPTER 1

'The Wall'

"Will you carry my backpack?" I softly asked. It was the question I never, ever wanted to ask anybody. Not even a Sherpa. Having to ask it felt almost like a blow to the gut. But the grim scenario I had been dreading for eight months had suddenly materialized.

It was October 18, 2012. I was lying sideways in the snow at approximately 17,300 feet on Thorung Peak near the top of the *Annapurna Circuit*. For the eight months since booking this trip to Nepal, I had been preoccupied with this very day. My task was very simple. I needed to—in fact, I absolutely had to—ascend another 500 feet to arrive at *Thorung La Pass*. If I could just make it there, it would be a 5,300 foot descent over the course of the following four miles. Every step downward would represent liberation.

"I thought I was gonna' die," is an exclamation we've all heard countless times, and probably even said ourselves. But let me be clear: I did NOT think I was going to die here. However, consideration of one's mortality was not reckless paranoia in this particular situation. After all, every guidebook and history of the Annapurna Circuit pointed out that an average of two trekkers per year die right in this immediate area, attempting to clear Thorung La Pass.

What kind of person dies on the spot like that? Do I fit the profile? Maybe it was overweight or out-of-shape trekkers. But the truth was that I had now seen hundreds, if not thousands, of trekkers since beginning the Circuit. And it was striking just how fit most of them appeared. In fact, right this very moment, as I lay immobilized in the snow in a state of low-level fear, one trekker after another streamed past me with various gaits.

The Appalachian Trail is America's trail of the masses, whereas the European multitudes head to El Camino de Santiago. But the Annapurna Circuit clearly attracted a different breed individual. Heck, it was in the Himalayas—the mecca of high altitude enthusiasts. And it is in Nepal. Something about that name has always had a mystical shudder to it, even though for most of my life I had really known only one thing about the country—*Everest*.

***

My question ("Will you carry my backpack?") was directed at the 24 year-old Nepali man sitting next to me in the snow. His name was Shankar Aryal. He was my porter. In truth, I had never even wanted a porter. But through a well-executed entrapment plan laid by a local trekking agency, as well as my own lack of resolution, a porter now sat right at my feet. And for the first time since we had been introduced, I was glad he was here. Very glad, in fact.

Shankar knew I wasn't on solid footing. Earlier today, as we had started up the mountain in the frigid, black, early morning hours, he had softly suggested, "Bill, I carry your backpack." But when he had reached for it, I had thwarted him and insisted, "No, no, I carry it." I have never considered myself a great long-distance trekker; but I sure as heck have been an avid one, having hiked many of the world's great trails. So perhaps there was some residual pride in play. Nonetheless, Shankar's offer had been comforting. Better yet, he had renewed it three more times as we had trekked this morning through the snow to ever-higher elevations and thinner and thinner air.

Speaking of elevations, the highest I had ever gotten before this trek was 14,500 feet, after summiting the very highest point on the American mainland, Mount Whitney. But last night I had slept at Thorung Phedi Base Camp, whose elevation was slightly higher than that of Whitney summit. And the climb this morning out of Base Camp had been steep and unrelenting. The bottom line was—in mountaineering lingo—I was not 'acclimatized' to this altitude. How could I have been? It was all completely new.

Nonetheless, until just a few minutes ago, my late night-early morning trek had had that buoyant feeling associated with a long-dreaded task being carried out with dispatch. Momentum and adrenaline had been on my side; morale had been high. But then *it* had suddenly happened. My thoughts went back to the long journey through the desert that I had undertaken on the Pacific Crest Trail. I would be moving along at a healthy clip, chugging water at regular intervals. But then, *it* would happen. I would suddenly realize that I was badly dehydrated.

Now it had happened again, only this time in a dramatically different situation. Just in the last fifteen minutes, I had begun feeling like somebody had strapped a heavy water tank onto my back that was taking on ever more water each step. My stride had gone from the confident, adrenaline-fed paces of the first three hours this morning to pigeon steps. Perhaps even worse, I had now begun to feel dizzy, which had caused me to plop down right here in the snow. Of course, there wasn't much of a mystery as to what had happened. I had hit the so-called '*wall*' of mountaineering infamy.

The numerous readers of Jon Krakauer's outdoor narratives have at least a cursory awareness of this phenomenon. Nonetheless, while I had known that ascending to high elevations was a deadly serious matter, the whole concept of 'the wall' had just been too abstract to gain much of my attention. How could a person be going along fine one minute, but then suddenly be immobilized the next? My experience had been that fatigue was more of a linear event. A person just gradually gets worn down. But at this elevation, the air has approximately 50% of the oxygen content of sea level. Combined with the great exertion expended in a rugged mountainous setting, and it all becomes a delicate dance.

My hope was that lying here in the snow would arrest this feeling of dizziness so that I could continue. It was hard to tell exactly how close the summit was because we had already hit multiple 'false summits' – a Himalayan trademark. But unless I was completely deluded, I had to be within 45 minutes of the Pass. Once at the top, there would be no celebration nor delay. I would immediately begin the 5,300 foot descent back to a more temperate zone. We had been repeatedly warned that brutal winds dominate Thorung La Pass by late morning. Because we had already faced bullying winds each afternoon in our trek to ever higher elevations, these reports had great credibility. So the need to get on with it dominated my thoughts.

'Don't panic' is the advice that mountaineers repeatedly voice. However, I had a long, rich history of panicking in fraught situations just such as these. This probably had to do with my late start in life as an outdoorsman (I had never even spent the night outdoors until age 44). But this time I really was determined to keep my act together. It was more than obvious that panic was the road to disaster. The nearest bailout point was at least a week away in the direction I had come from. Besides there were all the rickety suspension bridges and landslide zones that had turned me yellow time and time again during the course of the ascent. So I desperately didn't want to go back.

More than perhaps at any point in my life I needed to get off my bum right here and start trucking. *I just need 'a blow' first. Then I'll go.* But the only blow I seemed to be getting was my ever-heavier breaths. And true to high altitude mythology, a cracking headache was enveloping my skull.

***

"This break is not helping me get my breath," I reported to Shankar. Shankar's face took on an intent look – but he seemed to look about me, rather than directly face me. Needless to say, the cultural chasm is breathtakingly wide between a person from Macon, Georgia and a Nepali porter. Our relationship had been plagued at various points by communication problems. But they had never been more than an irritant until now. However, the strange thing – perhaps even eerie thing – was that I had begun to pick up a sense that I was not the only one worried. Finally, Shankar spoke up.

"Not good to stop long," Shankar he said. Those were not exactly enlightening words.

Shankar, himself, was not a Sherpa. That word is thrown around loosely by many tourists to the Himalyan region, and with great effect because of their legendary reputations for strength and agility. Sherpas are, in fact, an ethnic group specific to the Everest region. Nonetheless, Shankar was a Nepali porter. That tells you plenty right there. "All you Sherpas have lungs the size of aircraft hangars," one trekker had said half-seriously to a group of porters. But being a porter was also said to have much greater import than the simple fact of enhanced lung capacity.

"They're the toughest people in the world," trekker after trekker had told me. "They aren't afraid of anything." Personally, I find those two statements at least partly contradictory. However, I would say that in some basic ways Nepali porters are just flat-out different from your average mortal. We trekkers habitually tolerated their idiosyncracies because, at the end of the day, there was a bedrock assumption that a porter could handle any situation that might develop.

Now that time had come. I looked at Shankar. As many people as he had gotten over this pass, surely he had seen trekkers in various states of debility. His soothing tone of voice this morning in offering to carry my backpack had reflected that. Right now, with his client in a virtually helpless supine position, would be a logical time for him to renew his offer. But just to get the point across I sighed and hissed, indicating weakness, if not outright helplessness. But his face remained gnarled up.

"I've got a terrible headache," I said. But Shankar merely frowned and continued looking up ahead to where we needed to go.

"I'm getting weaker," I continued. But again, he did not break his silence. *Dammit, this exact situation right here is why we were almost universally advised to hire a porter in the first place.*

"Can you carry my backpack?" I finally blurted out (Note: I was carrying a backpack, but it was smaller than the one he was toting). I looked straight at him. My stare was met with an inscrutable indirection. *Maybe he doesn't understand my question.* His English was basic. But on second thought, *hell yeah he understands.* The very first two words in English virtually any Nepali boy learns are 'carry' and 'backpack'.

"Shankar," I said firmly and drew his attention "will you carry my backpack?" But yet again, my request was met with a pregnant silence. My confusion was clearing up. Shankar didn't want to carry my backpack. And it wasn't because he was either lazy or impudent. Nor was it that he looked scared. Heck, most Nepali porters would rather die before betraying any such timidity. Rather, Shankar appeared to be in a grim state himself. He was very thin-framed; I had noticed on occasion that he didn't have quite the bluster of the other porters.

"We go," he finally answered. Shankar wanted to get climbing again; he sensed there was trouble in lying right here. I did too. It's just that I wasn't sure if I was capable of going higher. But in a peculiar logic, continuing up seemed almost like the path of least resistance. I was miserable, cold, and weak. But I wasn't going to be able gain sustenance right here. Besides, the default position for most any trekker is to walk. We are creatures with an abiding faith that if you simply walk, things will ultimately work out for the best. They usually do. Almost always. "Let's go," I said quietly. Well, Shankar sure understood *that*. He jumped to his feet immediately.

Now, without trying to, my stride was reduced to my paternal grandmother's pigeon steps in the nursing home of her later years. I began to deliberately plant one foot right at the tip of the other. And all attempts at efficiently regulating breathing through the mouth, per my high altitude training, were quickly abandoned. I inhaled deeply. People we had passed on the way up this morning continued soaring past me. However, even these relatively strong souls seemed to have lost all camaraderie. At this altitude, you play for keeps.

After five minutes, even this zombie-like gait gave out. But taking a break had already been proven a failed option. I doubled over my two trekking poles. The only real strength I showed was that when I began praying, I found enough strength to not break my cardinal rule. I would never, ever pray for my life. And I did not do so here.

BILL WALKER

CHAPTER 2

The Third World

Well damn me for using that despicably presumptuous term, 'Third World'. What the hell am I talking about anyway? Actually, I love the Third World. Except, of course, when I hate it.

In 1995 I was wandering alone through Tacsquin Square in the center of Istanbul, Turkey. It was my first night in the country, and I was lonely. A Turkish man approximately my age approached me and said, "Hello." That was about the first word of English I had heard since getting off the airplane, and I responded positively.

"Hey, there is good club down the street," the man said. "Many foreigners go." Off we went and soon entered a medium-sized bar where we took a seat in the first booth. There was nothing terribly unusual about any of this. However, I soon noticed some very noticeable girls loitering over in the corner. Right away two attractive Caucasian girls approached our table to politely ask in broken English if they could join us. Hopefully, the reader will not be shocked to learn that I did not shoo them away. Not missing a beat, the bartender came up to ask, "Do you want to buy her a drink?"

"Would you like a drink?" I asked the girl.

"Yes, thank you," she said in a charming voice. Then, without hesitation she turned to the bartender to say, "Champagne please."

It didn't take a hardened skeptic to see this was all a little bit too good to be true. When the waiter brought a big bottle of champagne and placed it in front of this petite young woman, my suspicions were immediately piqued. "Could I have the bill please?" I asked the waiter.

"You pay when you leave," he quickly countered.

That left me uneasy. However, I soon fell into an enjoyable chat with the girl at my side. Unsurprisingly she was Russian. Many such beautiful eastern European women had been tricked and trafficked to Third World Countries in the wake of the Cold War. We discussed Gorbachev, *glasnost*, and Reagan. In fact, we were really connecting (or so my foolish damn male ego led me to believe) until the waiter appeared at the table again.

"Would you like to buy her a drink?" he asked again.

"She hasn't even begun this bottle," I answered. To my consternation he quickly summoned the two girls up and they walked back over to the corner.

"Please bring me the bill," I said peeved.

He soon returned with a slip of paper showing a bill of 200,000,000 Turkish lira. *Oh my God.* The exchange rate was 40,000 lira per one U.S. dollar, which had me doing a quick mental calculation. *Is this bill $50, $500, or $5,000?* It was $500. *Do I have enough money?* Suddenly I noticed I was surrounded by several swarthy-looking Turkish males, hovering over both shoulders. When I looked across the table at my 'buddy' who had led me here, he cheerfully said, "I'll pay half," and handed over a dubious-looking plastic card to the men. I pulled out my wallet and started anxiously peeling through U.S. dollars and Turkish lira to see if I had $250, as my 'audience' peered intensively at its contents. "You can pay in different currencies," the man perched just above my right shoulder helpfully said.

I finally came up with a total of just over $200, at which point these virtual abductors humanely decided to allow me to evacuate the premises, along with my mate (who didn't seem anywhere near as disconsolate as me). In fact, once we got back to the main square he quickly doubled back around in the direction of the club, undoubtedly to collect his commission for delivering a big, fat turkey to these henchmen.

I soon learned that I had fallen for one of the oldest tricks in the book. Several more times that night, other hucksters—some quite colorful—sympathetically approached me to see if they could relieve my boredom and loneliness. And the following day I hung out with an Egyptian who seemed virtually disabled he was in such a stupor at having been so thoroughly fleeced. "It happened so quick," he kept muttering.

Obviously I'm not alone. Adventurous travelers to parts yonder love swapping war tales of misfortunes endured (although I have noticed some tales of easy victimhood are so outrageous that people take years to finally cough them up). So why go to such countries?

The great thing about LDC's – Lesser Developed Countries (the now politically correct term) almost any visitor will tell you, is the people. Almost universally they are more charming than in more developed countries. If nothing else, that does bring up a great irony. We humans spend our lives striving for economic advancement in order to make ourselves less attractive as people. Obviously it's more complicated than just that. But international travelers habitually return from LDC's flush with tales of the hospitality of the locals.

***

I was very happy to finally see Kathmandu, Nepal on October 2, 2012. I'm nearly 7-feet tall and religiously exercise twice a day. Jet travel doesn't suit me in the least. Since leaving Atlanta, Georgia 32 hours back, I had been in the air a total of 23 hours, which was at least double my theretofore known capacity for air travel. Needless to say, I felt as ragged as I looked. And that was a problem because 'the game' begins the minute you hit the ground in a country like Nepal. Especially if you have no travel visa, hotel room, transportation arrangements, or trekking company.

Of the 100,000 tourists Nepal welcomes annually, approximately two-thirds are trekkers. In fact, trekking is by far the country's biggest industry, and October was the kickoff of high season. And wow what an impressive-looking group of people. I never had seen such a conglomeration of healthy-looking physiques of twenty-something males and females as what had piled onto our plane in Doha, Quatar, headed for Nepal. My old inferiority instincts had quickly resurfaced.

Unfortunately, the airport in Kathmandu didn't seem to have caught up with business. Back in Doha, the airport had been a shiny new building that reeked of efficiency. But not here in Kathmandu, which is the capital of a much poorer country. A dusty-looking building with amazingly little in the way of electronic gadgets greeted us trekkers. Seemingly random lines began forming at various counters. Not sure what was going on, I looked for one that had neither the most nor the fewest people queued up. An officious-looking lady walked by.

"Visa?" I asked, pointing to the line I was in.

"Yes," she nodded her head helpfully. That was a good sign—good English and no attitude. The visa system was completely manual, but I made it through in a half-hour. Now came decision time.

I had asked several of the people in the airplane where they were planning to stay in Kathmandu and how they were going to get there. Without fail their answer was, "I don't know. The trekking company is picking us up." *Why in the world would these Nordic gods hire a damn Sherpa. They look like a bunch of Winter Olympic athletes.*

From what I had read online and from Jon Krakauer's outdoor narratives, *Thamel* was the section of Kathmandu where all the trekkers and climbers hung out. There I hoped to quickly be able to plug into the planning and logistics grapevine that surely would be extant.

I passed a booth that said *Information*. For someone who had made so few plans it seemed logical to stop and inquire here. *Right?* Two males who looked to be in their early thirties quickly rose to their feet when they saw me leaning over their booth.

"Excuse me," I said in the clearest English somebody from Macon, Georgia can muster, "do you know any economical hotels where trekkers stay in the Thamel district?" A hardened traveler to these parts would probably have laughed at my question. Of course, they had some solutions for me.

"Yes, we have the perfect hotel," the older one replied. "My brother will drive you there."

"Is he here at the airport?"

"Yes, right outside."

"What is the price?"

"Twenty dollars."

"For both the room and the ride?" I clarified.

"For both."

"I'll take it."

It sure seemed like a good deal, although perhaps it wasn't a propitious sign that the man jumped up so enthusiastically to lead me out to his brother. When we exited the airport into the morning sunshine, I confronted the scene that had preoccupied me for days. No, not a majestic Himalayan vista that I was pining for. Rather, a total onslaught of humanity looking to 'accommodate' me.

On the far curb were scores of Nepalis, bunched tightly together, scanning every foreign-looking person who exited the building. And just to give you an idea, over the course of the next five weeks I was not to see a single Nepali who actually cleared six-feet in height. I had expected this would be the case and was braced for the virtual bedlam that ensued as I walked hurriedly alongside my driver.

"Hotel, hotel, friend, hotel, taxi my friend, taxi, trekking company, hotel," came frantic screams at me. In the dead-middle of the signs I saw a sign saying *Kathmandu Guest House*. Before leaving for Nepal, about the only bow I had made to conventional planning was filling out a form on the internet for the Kathmandu Guest House; it promised a room and a free ride at the airport. A Dutch trekker I had known from a previous hike had told me, "The Kathmandu Guest House is kind of like a clearing house for the whole Annapurna Circuit. You can arrange everything there."

But I had also read online chatter from trekkers that had basically said, 'Good luck', on someone actually waiting to give me a ride, or even having a room available. *Maybe I should have given them a chance.* I quickly thought about shunting the driver aside and making a beeline for the guy with the Kathmandu Guest House sign. But then it occurred that maybe I was fortunate to not have to make what would almost feel like a 'perp walk' with all the other sign-holders baying at me. Alas, my indecisiveness here would prove consequential.

The driver led me to a small compact car where another young man sat in the driver's seat. Over the next month, I would learn that this was very much the Nepalese way—everybody is in on the deal. I threw my backpack down sideways on the back seat and spread out beside it with my legs laid over the top for what would be an eye-opening trip into town. For a tourist's education begins quickly in a place like Nepal.

It took me a few minutes to realize the Nepalis drive on the left side of the road. Heck, my slow learning curve can be forgiven, if I may say so myself. A sizeable fraction of the cars heading towards us also seemed to be on our left (their right) side of the road. Immediately though, that most revealing of Third World Country—excuse me, Lesser Developed Country—habits, indiscriminate horn-blowing, reared its rude head. As best I could tell, 90% of the honking was done for the simple reason that the driver could do it. But the other 10% had a more salient purpose—avoidance of head-on collisions. The 'scenery', though, on this drive in from the airport was breathtaking. But not in the way of the Blue Ridge Parkway or Pacific Coast Highway. Rather, harsh, indescribable poverty was in our face all along the way.

A dozen years back on the way into New Delhi, India from the airport I had been jolted when children with forearms bent at perfect 90 degree angles had come up to the window of the taxi pleading for money. "Their parents break their arms at birth to make them more effective beggars," our tour guide had informed us. Later we would see children whose spines had been crushed at birth; they would crawl along the ground and attempt to grab foreigners and not let go until the flustered tourist coughed up money. Fortunately, I would soon learn the Nepali people are far too humane to engage in anything quite so macabre.

Having said that, Nepal was to be the only place I have ever traveled where the poverty is more deeply woven into its fabric than in India. Adults hovered around one-story grottoes, while children and animals ranging from dogs to bulls roamed the chaotic streets. Pushcarts powered by old men, animals pulling carts piled high with dung, and feces-filled streets were all part of the tapestry. The most jolting thing, though, was the number of people with masks covering their mouths. And it was not principally foreign tourists who were wearing them, but Nepalis. A dense, foggy pollution held the city in an iron group. When I asked the driver about this, he responded in an upbeat fashion: "During monsoon season when we get the fresh rains, people take them off." Glad to hear. The ironic truth was that the streets were swarming with bicycles, motorcycles, rickshaws, and the like—all the things that an ardent conservationist such as myself would advocate to control pollution.

***

"Do you have a trekking company?" the brother suddenly turned around to ask. I made a mistake. I told him the truth. I say it was a mistake. Who knows? It may ultimately have saved my life. But I would replay this moment in my mind countless times over the next few weeks.

Actually, websites, friends, and former trekkers to the Himalayas had almost universally suggested that I get a trekking company to provide me with a porter and/or guide. "Bill, don't be stubborn," my mother had repeatedly badgered me before I had left for Nepal. "Everybody gets a trekking company." Point well taken. When I had begun long-distance hiking in 2005 at age 44, this would have been an easy decision. But here in the fall of 2012, I was more 'invested' in a decision like this. After all, I had thru-hiked the 2,175 mile Appalachian Trail and done all but the impassable parts of the 2,663 mile Pacific Crest Trail, which runs from Mexico to Canada. Certainly nobody who has ever hiked with me would say I was an expert; nor would they say I was an egotist. Nonetheless, I had proven in the past seven years to be pretty dogged in making it from Point A to Point B, even when point B lay on the other side of a country.

I had often witnessed fellow hikers who had not given it their all in what potentially could have become the journeys of their lifetimes. Inexplicably, many would just start skipping sections; others just quit altogether. When I would see them afterwards – sometimes years later – there was usually a defensiveness, a palpable regret that they had not fully thrown themselves into the 'Great Outdoors'. I took pride that despite my modest ability, I had been an overachiever of sorts. And I didn't want to shortchange myself on the Annapurna Circuit.

"Why would I want a caddie?" I had colloquially answered these suggestions that I hire a Sherpa. And the idea that any of these thoroughbreds I had seen on the airplane would hire porters to carry anything other than maybe their jock straps was mystifying.

"No, I'm not using a trekking company," I responded to the two men in the front seat. Perhaps this would have been a propitious time for a white lie. Because the minute the words were out of my mouth, both of them immediately pulled out cell phones and start dialing, while intermittently flashing signals to each other. The brother then turned around to softly say, "Sir, a man will be meeting you at the hotel to discuss your trekking permit." *Permit*.

***

A volt of unease rippled through my jet-lagged body. I had read online that I would actually need to get two different trekking permits to do the Annapurna Circuit. While waiting in the line at the airport I had asked other trekkers about these permits; but invariably the response was, "My trekking company is handling that." However, I still held out hope that when I got to Thamel, I could hook up with those in the know about things like trekking permits, as well as the question of transportation to the beginning of the Annapurna Circuit.

We finally turned off one of the main streets and pulled up to a non-descript building that could have passed for a cheap hotel hotel in a backwater American town. Immediately people from everywhere were opening doors and reaching for my backpack. But I had already conceded some of my independence back at the airport by agreeing to this arrangement, so I clung to my backpack and transported it inside myself.

I also insisted on paying up right away out of fear that in the morning they would claim I had agreed to a much higher price than $20. However, I would soon learn that even this price was a rip-off compared to other similar hotels. But it was nothing compared to the mouse trap that awaited me when the two taxi conductors and the manager of the hotel introduced me to a nicely dressed, well-spoken man in this thirties who I later found out was from India (I would soon learn that Nepalis never tire of hyperventilating about the supposed depredations of Indian business people).

"My name is Vijay," the man said. "I would like to talk with you about your trip to the Annapurna Circuit."

"Can we do it later?" I replied sullenly. "I've been traveling for forty hours."

"We need to talk now," he held firm. "It can be difficult arranging permits."

This man's strategy was obviously predicated on the assumption that tourists are the most vulnerable when completely exhausted. And his modus operandi was holistic, because the theretofore polite drivers and hotel staff now began looking gravely at me. The place I craved—my bedroom upstairs—was seemingly off-limits.

Vijay proceeded to outline a numbingly complex process of obtaining the *Annapurna Conservation Permit*. In fact, several years back the Nepalese government had bowed to heavy lobbying from the trekking companies and passed a law that actually required foreign trekkers to hire a trekking company. But trekkers are a fiercely independent lot; all hell had quickly broken loose online, threatening a trekker boycott of Nepal unless the extortionate law was repealed. Finally, under intense pressure, the Nepalese government had backed down. But as a face-saving measure, they began requiring that trekkers get a second permit—the *Trekkers Management System* (TMS).

The whole setup and presentation here at the hotel was so obviously designed to overwhelm me that my stubborn instincts began to kick in. "Yeah, I'm going to talk with some other trekkers and see how to arrange the permits," I told Vijay.

"How do you plan to get to the beginning of Annapurna?" he quickly asked.

"I'll take a bus to *BesiSahar*," I answered. "Is the bus station near here?" At first he ignored my question. But after I repeated it, he predictably answered, "No, it is not."

"Have you ever walked in the Himalayas?" he wanted to know.

"No, but I have extensive trekking experience elsewhere." I was indeed holding firm. But the fact was that he had hit a sensitive spot. *Permits. Where? Buses. Where?* Kathmandu is huge and unwieldy.

"If you go alone," he said in lawyerly fashion, "there are certain issues you will face that have caused trekkers considerable problems."

"Such as," I replied. My impudent tone wasn't deterring him one bit and he went for the jugular.

"Are you familiar with the Maoists?" *The Maoists. Oh, my.* The Maoists, of course, are renowned around the world for populating mountainous regions of especially poor countries where they extort right-of-passage bribes from foreigners. Indeed, several years back, the Maoists had been very active in demanding wholesome bribes from Annapurna trekkers. But then a bittersweet event had occurred that ended up being fortuitous for trekkers. The Maoists gained majority control of Parliament. Seeing that their extortion policy was cratering tourism, the Maoists had announced a halt in demanding bribes from Annapurna trekkers. Or at least so I had read.

"But I heard they quit," I said in an almost pleading fashion.

"There are problems," he answered me in a funereal tone.

This son of a bitch. Yes, he was doing a good job putting me ill at ease. But he had pissed me off. I was ready to walk away. However, the only beachhead I had in this chaotic city of millions, 10,000 miles from home, was the hotel room I had paid for but had not been given the key to yet.

"The most important thing our guides can do for you is keep you from getting badly lost."

G#%dammit. I had been worried about *that* for a good while, also. Not worried sick. Just a concern. My previous hikes had always featured hikers with well-earned trail names, the likes of *Backtrack* and *Wrongway.* Heck, I had sometimes amazed my own self at the way I absent-mindedly missed turns and ended up having to retrace miles that I had veered off in the wrong direction. *What would happen if I did that in the Himalayas?*

"Do people get lost much up there?" I asked him. Boy I really know who to ask for information!

"It is often difficult at the very top, as you start the descent." But this time I had a fallback defense.

"If I feel like I need a porter, I will get one in *Manang.*" Indeed, I had read that almost every trekker took an acclimatization day in the mountainous village of Manang, which lay three days from the summit. Reportedly a trekker could just rent a porter for those three days only. But when I mentioned this to him, he was ready.

"Those porters are uninsured. If anything happens, like the porter getting sick or stealing your backpack—there have been instances of this—then you have lost your money." *Wow, he's good. Steal my backpack.* I gotta' admit, the possibility of such a trip-ruining theft had occurred to me.

So again he had landed a body blow. Better yet (for Vijay), he wouldn't be anywhere in sight when I quickly realized the Circuit was so well marked and populated that it was virtually impossible to get lost. Finally, Vijay played his trump card.

"Have you got reservations in any of the teahouses (where trekkers stay overnight)?" he asked.

"No," I answered confidently, "supposedly they are first-come, first serve. Plus I like to be flexible. I never know how far I'm going to walk until late in the day." Indeed, spontaneous decisions are one of the great things about long-distance hiking. And the Annapurna Circuit seemed like the Camino de Santiago pilgrimage in Europe—you could do it all on a shoestring. But not so quick.

"If you don't have a trekking company," Vijay said, "the teahouses will charge you a 23% food and lodging tax. It will cost you almost as much to do the Circuit without a trekking company." This immediately drew blood. *I won't save any money by carrying my backpack.* Of course, this also happened to be a flat-out lie. But I had no way of knowing it at the time.

Now it was time for him to throw his knockout punch. "It is high season. You will not be able to find rooms in many villages unless you have a good trekking company. Also, teahouses serve dinner first to the trekkers who have reservations. If they run out, you will not get any food."

Not get any damn food. It was time for me to face the truth –

this guy had effectively beat the shit out of me.

"Okay," I crumbled, "I might consider a porter. But I don't need a guide. How much will a porter cost?" Thus round two commenced.

I initially fared better in the second round than in the first. We agreed on a price of $300. But as the long-drawn out paperwork drew on and I was yawning uncontrollably, he came in with all kinds of late add-ons for porter transportation and other incomprehensible terms I didn't understand and was too tired to contest. The final price added up to $425 for 16 days. In a country where the average annual per capital income is $490 per year, I hadn't exactly earned the Henry Kissinger Award for negotiation. But he did have a consolation prize for my bruised psyche. He pulled a file out of a vanilla folder and said, "Look, this Frenchman here paid 800 Euros."

CHAPTER 3

Thamel

Fortunately, the frenetic streets of *Thamel* proved to be significantly more charming than this Indian-Nepali tycoon. But only marginally more friendly.

It was high season. The air in Kathmandu was pleasantly warm, with the sweet odor of incense and spices wafting through the air, along with the smoke from cooking fires, and even animal feces blending in the aroma. And, of course, the locals were in top form. All kinds of people approached to offer 'help'. Unsurprisingly, young men had various women in what they considered to be their 'inventory' (One knave even whispered "psss, psss, me young sister," from an alleyway as I passed by). Of course, this wasn't any big shock. This kind of human trafficking is a staple of life in many LDC's. And I'm certainly not any kind of saint. But there was a banality – a certain nausea – to the entire scene that made it plenty easy to walk away from.

"Friend, friend, do you smoke?" others wanted to know. *Smoke?* "I have hash." *Ah, hash.* How could I not have known. In Jon Krakauer's bestselling book, *Into Thin Air*, he recounts wandering through Thamel to buy some hash to help him cope with the tragedy he had just witnessed on Mount Everest. But I was not tempted by this either. However, apparently many people are. For every one hustler out there selling women, at least ten were peddling hash. And you've got to assume these street vendors know their market. A helluva' lot of these Euro-trekkers obviously imbibe hash while in Nepal. I pass no judgment.

However, I can honestly say that at no point did I feel as if anybody would ever attempt to rob, mug, or even kidnap me, as so often happens in exotic tourist destinations the likes of Rio de Janiero, Mexico City, etc. Other trekkers I spoke with universally agreed with this assessment. There really is just something about mountain people – which is ultimately what the Nepalese are – that makes them more pleasant to be around.

Thamel, with its ancient labrynth of crooked alleyways and serpentine byways, has long been a kind of exotic hybrid of medieval Asia. In the 1960's, it became a favorite haunt of Third World ramblers,

Chaos reigns in Thamel

low-budget travelers, hippies, and the like pouring through its bustling streets. The real danger, as best as I could tell, lay in literally being run over. Throngs of cars, rickshaws, cows, and taxis went barreling, trundling, and swerving through the narrow streets. And therein lay the rub. For there are no sidewalks in Thamel – none. You'd suddenly hear a blaring car horn and have to jump into the concrete gutter alongside other terrified tourists (Years of training has obviously inculcated the locals with steel nerves). Nonetheless, I have a long history myself as a 'streetwalker' in cities around the world. So I was determined to hang with the masses out on the street.

Reams of outdoor shops were packed to the rafters with name-brand gear. The prices were fantastic. I bought two Leki Trekking Poles for 400 Rupees (about $5) at one shop; two poles of the same brand in the United States would have cost almost $100. However when I chortled about this to some other trekkers, one hardened visitor informed me that everything sold in these shops was 'knockffs', assembled in a nearby town. He was almost surely right. But it was still a helluva' deal and a viable low-cost shopping option.

All in all, Kathmandu was a glorious display of humanity and I could feel the excitement building. At the Kathamandu Guest House where I relocated to for the second night, reams of foreign trekkers from around the world (French, Israelis, Germans, Russians, Chinese, British, Australians) were all buzzing on about the Himalayas and high elevations we were all headed off to.

My porter was to meet me at 6:00 in the morning, where we were to take the bus to the beginning of the world's premier mountain chain. But what I didn't know was that just getting to the starting point of the Annapurna Circuit would require a bus trip I will not soon forget.

BILL WALKER

CHAPTER 4

The Nepalese Way

For homecoming my freshman year in college, I took out a 6'2"
girl who easily outweighed me by 30 pounds, all of which invited
a cascade of idiotic jokes—"Amazon and Andre the Giant." While
working in Chicago as a commodities broker, I got set up with a
very impressive girl that I went out with for two years. But none
of these was as potentially significant as the blind date I stood
waiting for early in the morning of October 5, 2012 in front of the
Kathmandu Guest House.

Incidentally, I've also been stood up before on blind dates. A
quick ego bruise is sustained to be sure. But you live on to joke
with your friends about it the next day. However this 'blind date' I
had with a young Nepali man, Shankar Aryal, had greater import.
At 5:50 a.m. I stood in front of the hotel awaiting his arrival. *What
if he doesn't show up?* It occurred to me that I had absolutely no
recourse if nobody turned up here looking for me. Besides having
already forked over the entire purchase price for his services, he
was supposed to bring my two permits, as well as directions and
a bus ticket. To be sure, the previous night some veteran Euro
trekkers had assured me there was no reason to worry. "Porter is a
prestigious job in Nepal," was the unanimous sentiment. "He will
be there."

Indeed, at 6:00 sharp, a wiry-looking male bounded up the walkway to the hotel.

"Bill," he said.

"Shankar," I greeted him back. "Hello."

We shook hands and headed out to the main street, as I closely observed his walking stride. Shankar was on the slim side, and took long strides reaching outward with both legs.

When we got out to the street, a quick conversation ensued between him and a taxi driver. Then Shankar said, "Bill, backpack," and pointed to the backseat. I had heard that Nepali porters don't speak any English and was pleasantly surprised to learn that he did speak a bit.

"Shankar, how many times have you done the Annapurna Circuit?" I asked in the taxi. He continued looking forward with no expression, while my eyes stayed fixed on him.

"Eight," he finally said with no change in expression.

"Is Thorung La Pass very difficult?" I probed. His expression hardened a bit. "No," he answered tersely. "Not difficult."

However, no such comforting news awaited me at the bus station. The Annapurna Circuit begins 89 miles from Kathmandu, in the lowland village of *Besi Sahar*. I had been asking all kinds of people if there were any other way to get there besides the bus. Most unfortunately, the answer was 'no'. In fact, the more experienced travelers would furrow their brows and narrow their eyes at this question before saying, "No, and it's the local bus." *Local bus.*

I do not want to belabor the following point because this is an outdoor narrative. But just let me say this: extreme height is a major factor when traveling overseas, especially in Lesser Developed Countries. I remember getting on crowded buses while living in Mexico City and having to bend my upper body at 45 degree angles. In fact, the issue of height had been at the forefront of my consciousness in the months leading up to the trip to Nepal. And today was the day it would be a factor more than any other. Yet even with all this mental preparation, my heart sank when I saw what lay before us—a ramshackle-looking clunker of a bus that, frankly, was difficult to imagine making it very far into the mountains. However, young Nepali men were energetically going about strapping backpacks and other gear onto the top of the roof.

I hurried onto the bus and anxiously looked about for a place that would allow me to dangle my legs in some fashion. "Here," Shankar said, patting the very front seat. I plopped down and he sat right next to me. But then I remembered that I had asked Vijay whether the bus would have a bathroom. Honest to God, he had briefly looked like he was having to suppress laughter at the ridiculousness of my question before answering with a straight face, "No, they don't."

I rushed off to find a bathroom and resolved to carefully regulate my food and water intake during the day. Alas, when I got back to the bus, not only was it full, but backpacks had been stuffed between my seat on the front row and the driver's seat. A dozen or so porters and trekking guides were now all hunched up in squatted positions in the front of the bus. To my surprise, an especially muscular-looking man—actually he appeared more like a teenage boy—in a white tank top shirt jumped into the driver's seat. I was to watch this man-child very attentively for almost the entire day.

Three sturdy young men remained standing on the steps into the bus, with one literally hanging by his arm out the door (It was never closed the entire trip). These were the 'wingmen', which on this day 1 was to learn are integral to any Nepalese bus trip. Right before departure, these wingmen carried several barrels of God-knows-what onto the bus and rolled them into the aisleway. I looked around at the other passengers. Trekkers are a poker-faced lot, to be sure. But low-level looks of concern were creeping across their faces. The man-boy at the helm then cranked the bus up, and we began chugging down what appeared to be a major highway.

However, twenty minutes after departing we found ourselves completely stalled out on the side of the road. The driver immediately reached down and pulled a metal panel out of the floorboard, where the engine was revealed right in front of my eyes. For the next quarter hour he repeatedly attempted to crank the bus. Finally, he yelled something over to the wingmen, all three of whom immediately broke into full flight out of the bus door. "Let's get out," I motioned to Shankar and struggled to disengage myself from the seat. Others slowly filed out after us. Soon the three men came running back down a hill, each carrying a huge wrench. They immediately hit the pavement and without hesitation crawled up under the bus. For the next hour, Nepali males off the bus went running and flailing around, as we all tried to divine if they were actually making any progress. ("It's the starter." "No, it's a flat tire." "Hey, they're calling another bus to come get us.")

I noticed that my backpack seemed to have shaken loose from the rope. It was now angled down off the roof towards the near side of the bus.

"Shankar," I said anxiously, "my backpack is loose."

"Backpack?" he asked and appeared confused.

"Loose," I said and made a tightening motion. After some confused shouting he finally got two Nepali boys to climb up onto the roof, where they easily shook my backpack loose. After a moment of looking around, one of them grabbed it, hauled it over to the other side of the roof, and strapped it onto the top of another backpack. *It should be okay*. But I must not have been the only person concerned about our top-heavy bus. Two policemen soon pulled over and began intermittently pointing at the roof with stern looks. But the young men working on the bus just ignored them and continued scurrying around. Finally the driver got the engine to crank again, with clouds of black smoke fuming out of the exhaust. Rather than engage in any American-style high fives, the repair crew dutifully went about waving us back onto the bus. We headed off again.

***

The porters were now so tightly packed in that the driver was forced to edge over to the side of his bucket seat. But it wasn't like they were being hogs. Most simply did not have a seat. Rather they were bent to their knees in a crouch. In fact, on this day I was to realize that Nepali porters have a little-remarked upon skill, besides the one they're world-famous for. They are able to sit completely still for long periods of time as if they were in a telephone booth contest. Most of them would be stuck in these frozen positions for the better part of 13 hours.

"So how long is the ride to Besi Sahar?" I had specifically asked my friend, Vijay. "Five or six hours?" He had looked at me momentarily surprised – which qualifies as a *faux pas* for a con man. But he had quickly recovered and said, "Six." In this case, lying hadn't furthered his cause one bit because there was no other way to the starting line of the Annapurna Circuit.

Reading was an impossibility given the way the bus jostled around the mostly dirt roads. Instead, I stared straight ahead and focused on taking long, deep breaths. *This is a big day. Stay cool.* Occasionally I actually tried to dangle my feet out the bus window; but quickly I realized it was dangerous with so many vehicles blaring so closely by in both directions. Buses and trucks were everywhere on these mountainous dirt roads. The man-boy maneuvered the large black steering wheel with frequent sharp turns and even more frequent blaring of our horn.

To the naked eye, the prevailing law of the road was anarchy. Trucks and buses would be backed up in long, but poorly delineated, lines. Even on sharp mountainous turns we would be passing long lines of them, as I held my breath and tried to remain calm. But the trucks and buses coming from the opposite direction were also doing the same thing; at times this even resulted in our bus passing by other vehicles, with both of us in the wrong lane.

The three 'wingmen' standing on the steps of the bus, took turns hanging out the door. Every time our top-heavy vehicle leaned too far to the right (which is where the steep drop-off to the river was), they would all grab hold of something and lean out of the door to the left to balance the vehicle. They also maintained a steady dialogue with the driver, apparently about road conditions and driving strategy. Two different times our wingmen let out sharp, guttural sounds when trucks veered at us and then away. The porters up front would all jeer in tandem, and our driver would bring the bus to a halt. A Nepali-style mini-drama would then quickly unfold.

The wingmen would immediately jump off the bus and run over to engage the wingmen from the opposing vehicle in heated screaming matches, everybody making stabbing motions with their fingers in the air. A look of wounded pride – that most grievous offense to hard working people in poor countries – would be etched across their faces when they piled back onto our bus. But the damn truth was that the road incidents that led to these highly charged encounters didn't look much different to me than what was happening out there almost the entire time.

The drop-offs on our right side down to the river were harrowingly steep. Our bus, which never exceeded about 30 miles per hour all day, edged breathtakingly close to the edges. A quick Google will yield several results of just such deadly plunges into these cavernous gorges (although many crashes go unreported).

At various stops, vendors jumped on the bus offering up assorted fare. I actually wanted to sample a few of the items on offer. But as crowded as it was, I felt practically handcuffed and unable to retrieve my wallet. Another time, we passed through a small village, when the driver spotted a water fountain, bolted out of the bus with the motor still running, jumped in the fountain, and then ran back into the bus and drove us off. A few times I looked way down into the gorges, where I would see young children – five, six, seven years old – edging into the flowing river. But no parents were anywhere to be found. *This is a different country.*

Finally, at 6:00, eleven hours after boarding, the bus pulled into the dusty hamlet of *Besi Sahar* at the foot of the Himalayas. But when I hurriedly began to get off, Shankar put his hand out and quietly said, "Bill, no here." I anxiously began to question him. But a Canadian man behind me said, "He's right. Most people begin in *Bhule-Bhule* because of the traffic on this road." My stomach sank. I desperately – desperately – wanted out of this metallic canister.

"How far is Bhule-Bhule?" I asked the man.

"Eight kilometers," he answered.

Eight kilometers. That shouldn't be that bad. I reluctantly settled back on my sore romp. But if I had to do it over again, I'd hop off that bus there in Besi Sahar in a New York minute.

The road going into the mountains was quickly reduced to a bumpy jeep track that looked like it had been constructed during Genghis Khan's occupation. The bus lurched from side to side, while the driver used his great strength to ratchet the wheel back and forth. Yet at other times this man-boy showed a virtual surgeon's touch as he navigated between mountains on the left and steep drop-offs on the right. I was seated on the right side and – to quote my late father – there wouldn't have been a greasy spot left of me had the bus slid just a foot off track on the wet surface. My medium-grade level of worry throughout the day morphed into something just shy of outright terror.

In any event, all's well that ends well (I guess). We alighted in Bhule Bhule, Nepal at 8:00, 89 miles and 13 hours after boarding this morning. Often it is the unpleasant experiences that teach you the most about a place. This 'full-immersion' Nepalese-style day had shown me both the high-energy and feral side of Nepal which foreigners have long found so enticing.

And let me say one final thing about that man-boy (and now my first Nepali hero) who guided that packed bus through so much treachery. It was the single most impressive day of work I have ever seen a human being put in.

CHAPTER 5

Heading Up

"They don't eat until about 11:00," the Australian across the table said without hesitation.

"Oh, okay," I replied. We were having breakfast at 7:00 in the morning in Bhule-Bhule, Nepal. I was wondering why no porters seemed to be partaking.

Of course, the previous night we had arrived in this small village well after dark. Like most people, I had been very curious as to just what the 'teahouses' – where trekkers stay every night – would look like. One hiker had expressed nostalgic hopes that they would be similar to those idyllic teahouses astride mountaintops, with geishas, manicured gardens, and spotless padded dining areas. Not shockingly, *he* was let down. They were basically a row of ten or twelve concrete block rooms. Each room had two elevated rectangular boards with a thin mattress on top. In a separate stone hovel there was a drain toilet in which to urinate and crap.

"There, Shankar," I had said when the owner of the teahouse had taken me to a room. "You can take that bed right over there." But my response had drawn a quizzical look from the owner; Shankar had hesitated as well. Porters traditionally eat and sleep apart from trekkers in tight quarters. Very tight, in fact, as I would later see from some sneak peeks. But I fancied myself as a 'porter's trekker', if you will. Needless to say they had a lot to teach me. The less distance between my porter and myself, hopefully the faster my learning curve.

Obviously the bed was not long enough for me. In fact, for months I had wondered just how big of problem the beds would be, and expected the worst. Through hard-won experience, I've learned that in cases where the bed is hopelessly short – like this one – the best thing to do is just chunk the mattress on the floor. Using my backpack as a pillow effectively lengthensd the bed. Fortunately there was sufficient floor space to do this sleeping ju-jitsu. But soon after getting the whole thing jerry-rigged, the owner had walked by and gone into a minor panic.

He had quickly and sharply interrogated Shankar, who defensively pointed me. Soon he had loudly summoned the other members of his teahouse crew. At first I had been worried that he might be angry that I had thrown the mattress on the floor. But actually it had been just the opposite. Two sturdy young males came rushing into the room, removed the frame of the bed, and placed it into the courtyard, to give me more room for my makeshift floor bed. To be sure, their intentions had been good. However, when word had leaked out, trekkers from France, Austria, Israel, and various other countries had spilled out of their rooms to marvel at my sleeping arrangements, and in a couple cases had even run back to their rooms to retrieve their cameras. Fortunately, I've long since learned to roll with the punches on this issue.

What did actually bother me, though, was that Shankar was now waiting hand and knee on me at breakfast. Suffice it to say that being treated like royalty just ain't my cup of tea. And since he was the one who was going to be carrying my backpack, some nutrition for him seemed like a good idea.

I had recently read an article reporting that of Nepal's 26 million people, 24 million of them get by on two meals per day of vegetable curry (which they eat by hand). I made a mental note to plan on taking a break around 11:00 this morning, on the assumption that my porter would be ravenously hungry.

***

Now came the awkward part. Most people would say – and I would staunchly agree – that carrying a backpack is an integral part of long-distance hiking. Shankar now went about purposefully adjusting the various straps of my backpack to fit his frame. Unsurprisingly, he looked like he knew exactly what he was doing.

Shankar also had a smaller backpack for carrying his own belongings. If mine weighed 30 pounds (13.5 kilos), his weighed perhaps 13 pounds (6 kilos). "Hey," I suddenly said, "I'm going to carry your backpack."

But as I reached down to pick it up, he said, "No." Looking alarmed, he put out an arm and said, "Not good." However, I was I was uncomfortable enough with the whole thing that I decided this was the place to draw the line.

"Yes, I am carrying this backpack right here."

Off we went, neither of us particularly happy about this particular portage arrangement, although for different reasons.

Immediately I was confused. Everybody else seemed to be going in one direction, down a hill and over the river, while we headed straight up a road. "Hey, Shankar," I said, "trekkers going there." He looked down at them with a confused look. But then he said, "No, this way." I followed on his heels. Following a Nepali porter seemed like a safe bet.

Things changed quickly. Almost immediately I began panting as the Annapurna Circuit (APC) started up the face of a steep hill.

To our left, an aged woman trudged down a steep embankment with a full basket of wood on her back. It was difficult to guess this woman's age given the lack of modern cosmetics amongst the general population in Nepal. But it would be the first of many examples I would see of elderly ladies – sometimes severely elderly – doing backbreaking work. *I want a photo of her.* But then I realized my camera was in my backpack which was riding on Shankar's shoulders. To take a photo would require halting him in full march, having him remove the backpack, and then me digging my camera out and snapping a shot, before repeating all these steps in reverse. Like many westerners I had a bit of an inferiority complex around these Nepalese porters. I didn't want to bother him with any trivialities. So I forewent the photo op.

The sun came out early, as it almost always does in the Himalayas during trekking season. The nighttime chill rapidly gave way to a tropical aroma of flowers and mud and grass. Better yet, I was soon sweating profusely, an almost rhapsodic feeling after yesterday's horrible journey. But because we were headed to ever-higher elevations, it seemed desirable to economize on bodily sweat that would then chill me in the Himalayan nights.

"Shankar," I said, "I need to take off some clothes." I make these kinds of layer adjustments habitually when carrying my own backpack. Sometimes I will put on and take off the same item several times in the same day (Shankar himself would almost always wear the same item all day). But now I was defensive about it, not feeling the freedom to interrupt him at my whim.

Shankar set the backpack down and I began fumbling through its contents. The fruits of months of neurotic shopping to get ready for the Annna Purna Circuit—a heavy Icelandic sweater, two sets of long-johns, a rain jacket and pants, heavy sox, balaclava, neck warmer, scarf, and a wool hat came pouring out of the tightly packed stuff sacks. Immediately I was embarrassed and hurriedly stuffed the contents back in. *'What a wimp this guy is'*, he must be thinking, *needing so many clothes.*

Just in the short time we were stopped here, a group of three other porters had come charging up this escarpment. Oddly though, they had no trekkers at their side. And instead of mere backpacks on their shoulders, they had huge baskets filled with multiple backpacks tied down tightly by rope. *Who are they?*

"Wow, look at that," I exclaimed to Shankar. "How much weight? Fifty kilos (110 pounds)?"

"Less," he quickly said.

"Not much less."

'Move aside, folks. I'm 100% loaded.'   "Less."

Okay, maybe a little hyperbole on my part. But another human emotion seemed to enter the picture there as well. An unexpected one—a bit of defensiveness, if you will, on Shankar's part that these other Nepali porters were carrying more than him. For a Nepali male, carrying things is their virtual *raison d'etre*.

***

"It's like seeing the Rockies for the first time." I've heard that same analogy used to colorfully describe things as varied as federal budget deficits and skyscrapers, to feminine physiques. And to be sure, the Rockies inspire awe.

But when I finally cleared the first precipice on the Annapurna Circuit and beheld what lay directly out in the distance, I was staggered by an alpine scene the likes of which I had never before had the privilege to witness. The beginning of the Annapurna *massif* came immediately into sharp focus. Right away I was looking at two mountains that cleared 25,000 feet (7,700 meters), placing them among the top 20 peaks in the world. By comparison, the highest point on the American mainland, Mount Whitney, measures 14,494, and Mount McKinley (Denali) in Alaska has an altitude of 19,500 feet.

Down below – way, way down below – suddenly brought into sharp relief, were the surging rapids of the Marsyangdi River. In fact, we would be following this very river higher and higher into the mountains each day, as it wound through several climatic zones, until we would finally get very near its ultimate source. And so, eight months after booking my flight, several months of painstaking shopping in preparation, 23 hours in the air, 13 more on a dreadful bus, and now suddenly the whole effort seemed worth it.

But when I looked to the far side of the river, only a couple hundred meters away, trekkers I had met on the bus yesterday were traipsing along the banks on the far side of the river. What's more, their route appeared undulating and scenic, and with a steadily higher elevation than the road where we stood on this side of the river. As a matter of fact, we had not yet seen any trekkers on our side – only baggage porters carrying equipment for large groups.

"Trekkers, over there," I pointed out to Shankar. He briefly looked, but shrugged his shoulders. Then I asked, "*Ghermu?*" This was the first significant village listed in my guidebook. Indeed, a stately looking village of one story buildings lay perched on the bluff on the far banks, soon followed by a dazzling waterfall. Immediately I wished I was with all the trekkers over there.

"Is there any way we can get to the other side?" I asked Shankar, pointing at Ghermu.

But to my surprise, he answered, "No, other side more climbs."

He doesn't want to do it because it's more difficult?

***

Finally we came across a few small hamlets on our side. It was at least good to know that we trekkers had some flexibility as to where to stay. But I didn't see any customers, which put me off. I've long since learned that the big issue on any trip of whatever sort is the people, and whether or not you get to know some interesting personages.

With this in mind, I didn't want to stop at one of these small roadside stands, even though I was hungry and Shankar was probably famished. Finally though, we came to a cluster of buildings, one of which included a large RESTAURANT sign.

"Is this a good place?" I asked Shankar.

He shrugged his shoulders, and I decided to enter.

Like many foreigners, I get very neurotic over what I put in my stomach in foreign countries – especially in a country like Nepal which is really, really foreign. I had already decided I was going to drink bottled water the whole way. But this also meant I would be paying a higher and higher price every day of the ascent.

I felt hot and tired, which was to be expected. But now my throat felt sore which had me despondent. Worse yet, I felt like I might be running some fever. Even with my relative lack of true, bona-fide high-mountain experience, I knew that fever was the one thing you absolutely had to avoid while ascending.

In Kathmandu, I had recovered nicely from the marathon flight. But then I had gotten on that bloody bus. Being tensed up like that for so many hours had been a flat-out assault on my immune system. I probably should have taken the full day off today to recover from the horrific bus ride, just as I had done in Kathamandu after the long flight. Now I was in the bucket. And I was also deep in the mountains, and only headed higher.

I sat down in the empty restaurant and ordered some chicken-fried rice, the first of many dishes I would consume of this standard Himalayan fare. However, I still felt sullen afterwards and decided to order some vegetable soup and top it off with Advil. I then lay there for over an hour with my head down on the table. Already I was wondering whether to turn around and head back to lower elevations, or keep on ascending.

But at the end of the day, my great instinct was to walk. "If in doubt, walk," I have often told people. "Let the bad air out, and bring the good air in." Off Shankar and I went.

"How far to the next village?" I asked Shankar.

"250 meters (800 feet)," he answered.

What? Actually, this was the way they judged distances in Nepal. I kept asking "How far? How many kilometers?" But nobody spoke in those terms. It was all about elevation. After a while, this began to make more sense.

Late afternoon journeys are usually my favorite. With no need to conserve energy, you can just let it rip. Rarely do I take breaks this time of day. But as we ascended up a long, steep stairway towards our destination, I was unable to gain the customary momentum. My body and spirit were flagging. Finally we got to the top of a hill where the village of *Jagat* appeared in the distance.

Most such tiny pueblos are simply pass-through points to be marked with a cup of tea before moving on. And to be sure, I wasn't expecting to get to know this Maoist stronghold anywhere near as well as I eventually would.

CHAPTER 6

Staying Put

"Bill, this one," Shankar said, pointing at a teahouse on the right as we entered town.

However, I wasn't going to be so pliable. I had read many stories on the internet warning of porters and guides steering trekkers to teahouses where they had 'sweetheart deals'. Nor was I going to take one single step more to a higher elevation on this Annapurna Circuit before shaking the illness that was now enveloping me. The first order of business was to find a place that was not just comfortable, but also warm.

I dropped the backpack I was carrying at Shankar's feet and took to my heels around the village of Jagat for a quick inspection of what bedrooms were available. The local families that owned and ran the teahouses stood there befuddled as I ricocheted in and out of rooms. Finally, I found one with two beds that I could marry together. Better yet, the sun streamed into the large glass windows from the west, meaning I could probably keep the room warm for a while at least. Heck, the bathroom in this tea house even had a toilet seat, which I wouldn't be seeing again for a couple weeks.

"What price?" I asked an immaculately-dressed teenage girl showing me around, who also happened to be the owner's daughter.

"What price you like?" she asked to my surprise. *She's asking me!*

"What is normal?"

"One hundred and fifty (Less than two dollars)."

"I accept."

"Shankar, I'm going to have to stay alone tonight," I informed him. I hated setting myself apart from the porters and guides. But he nodded his head and headed off to find out where the porters slept (the kitchen).

The room was warm enough to relax my muscles, and I was able to fall asleep for a couple hours. However, I woke up feeling weak and chilled. I had a full-fledged, Nepalese bus-induced virus.

When I descended the stairs of the teahouse down to the patio where the other trekkers were gathered it was as if some *Yeti-like* freak (Nepal's version of *Big Foot)* had appeared. But, for once, the incredulous stares I got weren't principally because of my height. Rather, it was because of all the layers of clothes I was wearing to protect myself against any nighttime chill.

The crowd staying at this teahouse tonight was predominantly French.

"Are you ill?" one middle-aged man asked in a concerned tone.

"Yes, a bit."

"Well, let me get you some tea. Or do you prefer a glass of red wine?"

Of course, every American who has ever traveled abroad seems to have their favorite horror story about mistreatment by the arrogant French. Tales of rude waiters in Paris are virtual souvenirs. But I've learned that there is much more to the story. Like most people, the French get along well with people doing things that they respect. And what the French respect is people doing outdoor treks and traveling to forbidden parts of the world, sampling unknown cultures.

I had already noticed that there were more French on the Annapurna Circuit than any other nationality. And for very good reason. This particular area was the scene of one of their great moments of glory.

***

Edmund Hillary and Tenzig Norgay's 1953 summit of Mount Everest will remain forever in the annals. And deservedly so. However, three years before their epic ascent, in a mountain range approximately 90 miles to the west of Everest, a feat occurred that most mountaineers consider at least on par with it, if not any human effort ever.

In the spring of 1950, a French climbing party was given a permit by the Nepalese government to climb either Dhaulagiri (26,975 feet) or Annapurna I (26,540 feet). Maurice Herzog and Louis Lachenal were chosen to lead the mission. Since the two mountains are only 21 miles apart, they decided to head up Dhaulagiri first, but with the flexibility to divert to Annapurna I if they found a friendly route. A Buddhist monk that they came across in the high mountains eventually prophesied, "Dhaulagiri is not propitious for you. It would be best to give it up and turn to the other side." They followed suit, but were immediately amazed at the jaggedness of the ridge along the range.

The group received reports that the monsoon had already hit India, and would engulf the Himalayas within days. Further, they were deafened by the roar of continual avalanches. The first group of climbers turned back at Base Camp IV, and Herzog and Lachenal passed them on the way up. Lachenal was deathly worried about frostbite. Finally he asked Herzog what he would do if he turned back. Herzog answered that he would continue regardless. "Then I will follow you," Lachenal said, much to Herzog's relief.

Ultimately, the twosome (a Sherpa declined the final ascent) made a dash for the summit wearing light boots and without supplemental oxygen. "Everything was a struggle of mind over matter," Herzog later recalled. A fierce and savage wind tore at them as they got to the summit of Annapurna I. "The precipices on the far side, which plunged vertically down beneath us, were terrifying, unfathomable," he later wrote. "But never had I felt happiness so intense, yet so pure." Most unfortunately though, he lost his gloves up on the windy summit, leading to the eventual loss of all ten fingers.

The descent was quite simply a race against catastrophe. Delirious with pain, Herzog was eventually carried on porter's backs down to Base Camp and then placed in a wicker basket and carried all the way to India on steep, muddy trails. Finally they were able to catch a train through the Indian plains, with the expedition doctor systematically removing Herzog's gangrenous fingers and toes, and tossing them off the train as they went. Lachenal's toes were also eventually amputated.

Herzog and Lachenal returned home to France to heroic welcomes. Herzog then recorded to a scribe what many consider to be the greatest outdoor adventure book ever; over 12 million copies of *Annapurna* have been sold. Later Maurice Herzog went on to become the French Minister of Youth and Sport, and mayor of Chamonix.

Now just to be sure, the *Annapurna Circuit* that we were walking cannot be spoken of remotely in the same terms as climbing to the summit of Annapurna I. In fact, to this day Annapurna I is considered by many expert climbers to be the most difficult mountain in the world to climb. Thirty-eight percent of the people who have ever attempted it have died, which is a mortality rate greater than either Mount Everest in Nepal or K-2 in Pakistan.

Nonetheless, the French deserve credit in making the Annapurna Circuit one of the most popular treks in the world.

***

"What would you like for dinner?" the owner asked.

"Soup," I replied tersely.

A palpable look of consternation came across the face of this man about town. Out of my bedroom window, I had seen him laughing it up with other locals up on main street. And by the way they had all been throwing their hands up in jocularity, I got the impression they might well be talking about the *Cyclops* (me) who had just descended on town. Many of them would have probably never even left this provincial, Maoist-dominated village. So who could blame them? But now all he would be able to report to his buddies is that I had eaten a bowl of soup.

However, there was also a more direct explanation for his disappointment. Many teahouses had signs prominently posted informing trekkers that they were expected to eat dinner onsite. If you ate elsewhere, there would be a 500 rupees fine. The low room price was almost like a teaser; the food was priced multiples higher. Further, I suspected that the porters and guides got to eat and stay for free. So for things to work out for the teahouses—and this was their high season after all—they needed to make money off the kitchen.

Since it looked like I might be in town a while, I needed to develop some goodwill. So I ordered some tea and fried rice along with my soup. Alas, I was only able to take a few bites before pushing the plate aside, a sure sign I really was in the bucket.

The well-groomed daughter cleared my mostly full plates and then returned with a stethoscope to take my pulse. She looked like she knew what she was doing, so I just sat there intently watching her.

"One hundred thirty," she finally said.

"What is normal?" I asked.

"One hundred ten."

"How bad is 130?"

"Not so, so bad," she softly said. "But German man have high pressure last week and he go back down."

That sure got me thinking.

Fortunately, the conversation with the French went better. This particular group consisted of eleven middle-aged males, along with one man's daughter in her twenties. Unsurprisingly, her English was the best of the bunch. She had a certain confidence about her, having trekked in the Himalayas in her late teens without either a guide or porter. Better yet, these French like to have a good time. And they don't have to spend a fortune doing it either, unlike us Americans. These package trips that many Europeans take to Nepal, including a porter, guide, meals, and lodging, can actually be quite reasonable, if arranged in advance.

"We want you to walk with us tomorrow," the girl said.

My stomach sank. I would love to have gallivanted along with them. But since I could only eat a few bites of light food, it would be reckless to head directly to colder, thinner air tomorrow. "Just see how you feel in the morning," one non-descript man suggested with a palpable look of concern on his face. "You will probably know if you have to go back down."

I headed back up to the bedroom. From there I was rocked to sleep by the pleasant lullaby of French hymns that went on for the next hour or so.

***

A sightseeing tour of Jagat is bound to be short-lived, unless you are mighty industrious. I had woken up well up after everyone had departed. After a light breakfast, I wandered aimlessly up the main dirt road. It did not come as a total surprise that there were more animals than humans in town. In fact, most of the food is brought up by horses and donkeys.

Annapurna Circuit draws trekkers from around the world.
For the most part it is a balanced routine.

As I headed back to the hotel after walking the 200 or so meters to where the town gave out, I saw a large oncoming caravan. Packs were strapped on to the sides of the animals. I moved over to give the horses and donkeys safe passage. However, as they were streaming by, one donkey in the middle of the pack edged just a little bit out from the center and *whack* – smacked me with its side pack. Whether it was full of eggs, candy bars, tea bags, spaghetti, tuna, or water – all the things that a western trekker like myself demands – I was not able to discern. Another trekker happened to be passing by right at the point of impact, and was unable to suppress a comical laugh. After regaining my footing and coming to my senses I did the same, only to see a black bull walking in my direction. But heck, as much of the contents of these animals' side packs as I was to consume the next few weeks, perhaps it all served my gluttonous western ass right!

Back at the lodge, a solo Norwegian girl had stopped in for lunch. By this point, I had become lonely and was glad to see she was extroverted.

"You've got the advantage on the Annapurna Circuit," I suggested, "being from Norway." She didn't disagree. And when I told her about my illness, she became quite voluble.

"I have an extensive background in high mountaineering," she said in impeccable English. "It is absolutely essential that you take at least two days right here. If you try to go higher with your fever, you can expect to be sick for two months after the trip is over."

In a proverbial sense, I was a pretty 'easy lay' right now— desperate for advice and bound to believe anything I heard. And so I was a good patient and hung out in this Maoist village for two full days, as trekker after trekker from all over the world marched in and out of town, to my great envy.

CHAPTER 7

Shaky

I couldn't believe my eyes. A Nepali boy – perhaps he was even a man – looked at me with a look of hate flushed across his face. But on second thought, his visage may have been more one of horror, like he had just come upon a monster from the deep. Whatever the case, it scared the hell out of me.

Shankar and I had finally left Jagat after my Scandinavian-prescribed two-day recuperation in Jagat. Both of us seemed afflicted with mixed emotions. He had taken a shine to the owner's beautifully dressed, impeccably mannered daughter. But the Nepalese caste system, being what it is, the owner had noticeably begun to cast a disapproving eye at my porter. One veteran trekker told me that guides hold a much more exalted status in Nepalese society, because they are required to speak English and interact with foreigners. There must have been something to this; Shankar was soon speaking of his deep desire to improve his English and become a guide. I resolved to try to help him.

Meanwhile, I had closely questioned the owner about what lay ahead. "Are there any bailout points from the Annapurna Circuit?" I had specifically asked.

"No," he flatly said. "Maybe you could catch a ride back down on the jeep road."

He had also specifically advised us to follow the road out of town. "It is easier than the other side of the river," he had said.

But after following the road through *Chamje*, this Nepali boy, or man—it was difficult to tell—had rushed at me with his feet staggering the closer he got. It looked like he was trying to attack me. His eyes looked like they were practically popping out of his head. It is worth noting that hash and heroin production thrive in these isolated mountain regions.

I jumped back as this man came nearer. He had his hands out like he was rushing the quarterback in football. The very last thing I was looking do in Nepal (or anywhere else for that matter) was to get into a fight. So I continued retreating and started yelling, "No, no,", while wildly stabbing the ground in front of me with my two trekking poles. Shankar, who was about as thin as me, grabbed me by the arm and led me away from him.

As it ended up, the road that we had been advised to follow was closed, and a bunch of males had been standing around it. Perhaps it was just this fella's job to keep people off of it and he had fulfilled his task overenthusiastically. In any event, I would notice all along the way that each and every Nepali has a deeply abiding devotion to his or her tasks. Lazy people are simply unheard of in this part of the world.

The diversion we took would end up being much more eventful than the road anyway. And throw in just a touch of terror as well, if you just happen to be acrophobic. For we headed along a ridge and then down a steep bank towards the crashing river. On the opposite side of the river, a thundering waterfall came roaring out of the mountains (the Annapurna Circuit seemed to almost randomly serve up such delights). But to arrive on the far side near the waterfall meant I would need to cross my first suspension bridge in Nepal. I had thought long and hard about the cold and altitude before coming to Nepal. But suspension bridges had never even occurred to me.

Shankar and I followed a big group of Israelis to the bridge. They all piled on without any ado and started across. When they got halfway across, everyone pulled out their cameras, and started snapping shots of the tumbling rapids. I waited, because I didn't want anybody disrupting my balance on the swinging suspension. But by the time the Israelis had all cleared the bridge, a large herd of pack animals had appeared on the far bank. They also began edging down towards the bridge. *Are these animals able to negotiate this swinging suspension?* I watched in admiration as, one by one, a dozen-and-a-half horses and donkeys slowly, but surely, stepped onto the suspension bridge and negotiated it without incident.

Perhaps all this routine traffic across the bridge should have engendered confidence. But something closer to the opposite seemed to be the case. And to my consternation, by the time the animals had arrived at our end, another group was approaching the bridge from our side. So I tentatively started across, figuring my learning curve had better be steep. The guidebook said this was a Swiss-built suspension bridge; but I wondered whether *that* should be taken with a grain of salt. Individual panels of the wooden floorboards were missing in various parts. Perhaps worse, the two wire sides of the bridge came up somewhere on my upper thigh, compared to most everybody else's tummy. *If I lose my balance, is this flimsy, low-hanging wire going to save me?*

The obvious thing to concentrate on was keeping my center of gravity as low as possible. This meant bending my knees in an awkward deep crouch. I knew people would be jumping on behind me while I was in the act of crossing, and was ready for the immediate jolt. Indeed, soon after my first tentative steps, I felt footsteps hitting the panels from behind; they quickly were right on my back. *I'll be damned if I'm going to edge over to the side of this thing so they can pass me.* A couple minutes and plenty of lactic acid later and I had cleared the Marsyangdi River for the first of many times.

We began snaking up a mountain when we heard the sound of bells that would become so familiar. Soon another caravan of donkeys with empty satchels (after making deliveries higher up) came over the hill. You honestly wonder how a shepherd is able to maneuver these large animals up and down such steep, rocky slopes. Surely there are some horrific accidents. We stood there on a steep hillside for ten minutes as one enormous donkey after another negotiated the 90 degree right turn and then sharp descent. Any time, an animal momentarily hesitated, the shepherd let out a deep, guttural, "Arghhh," – a sound any Nepali boy could probably mimic in his sleep – and the pack animals would move steadily on.

The sun came out as we began ascending steeply through the forest. But I was still weak and felt a slight chill again. *Play it smart.* When we completed a steep climb and came upon a shady tree, I said, "Here, Shankar." There I took some Ibuprofen to stem any fever and drank an entire liter of bottled water to preempt any dehydration.

Hordes of trekkers from all over the world – just the kind of environment I like – streamed by. I love being in the action and chatting with the diverse cast of characters on an exotic journey like this; but now I was reduced to passively sitting off to the side with Shankar guessing the nationalities of the passers-by.

After a half-hour, I signaled I was ready to march again. Soon however we were ascending steeply up a jagged incline, and I was drenched in sweat – not exactly what the doctor had ordered. *Is this what the Annapurna Circuit is going to be like?* But finally, after a series of 50 degree ups-and-downs hopping off large rock gardens, the terrain sharply changed.

We looked down into a broad valley, where the river moved at a lazy pace, compared to its theretofore crashing rush. The village of Tal appeared in the distance, on the right banks of the river. *This place at least looks habitable.* The jagged path of the morning gave way to an easy glide into Tal.

***

Welcoming approach to Tal

The key to any peoples lies in their geography. A quick glance at Nepal's location on the map yields the conclusion that it is a precarious piece of real estate, to say the least. The country lies sandwiched between the two colossi, India to the south and China in the north. The Indian Hindu influence (Shankar was a Hindu from a rural farming area) appears strongest, especially in the low-lying areas. But the further one climbs into the Himalayas,

Chinese and Mongol racial characteristics become easily visible, the Mongols having invaded and moved across western China for millennia. The founders of Tal, that we were now entering, were an especially hardy Mongoloid people called the *Gurungs*.

We wandered down the main street of this village, passing stray horses and cows. Perhaps you could say Tal afforded us passersby a glimpse of the *Wild, Wild East*. I was pleased to see a long line of hotels to select from, and trekkers sat there enjoying themselves over lunch on the patios of these establishments. But when Shankar started walking into one of them, I said, "No, no, let's see who's here." I was still trying to get a grip on the essence of this Annapurna Circuit and its participants.

"Bill," I heard some people yelling out and waving me towards them. It was a French Canadian group who had stayed at the teahouse in Jagat last night.

"*Namaste,*" I yelled out.

"*Namaste,*" they all yelled back. "Come try the spaghetti fried rice."

I walked over and sat down with them for lunch.

"Are you going to stay here or continue?" one lady in the group asked me.

"I want to continue," I said. "But I'll see how I feel after lunch." Shankar again rushed around felicitously taking my food order. *I don't like this. I am not a sultan.* Unfortunately, after struggling through the spaghetti plate, I felt weak again. The afternoon winds in the Himalayas had begun gusting and my phobias started to set in. The nice Canadian group headed on.

When Shankar emerged from the kitchen, he picked up my backpack and said, "Ready, Bill."

"Well, let's go see what's going on with everybody else," I filibustered.

However, that may not have been a good idea. For as we got out on the long, dirt passageway through town, seemingly all the trekkers I had exchanged pleasantries with on the trail this morning were dutifully hoisting their backpacks to continue on to *Dharapani*. Shankar went over and chatted with a couple of porters, whose trekkers were packing up. Again, my every instinct was to be part of this crowd; but the bottom line was I still felt weak. The trump card in my decision was geography. You simply can't fuck around with the Himalayas.

"Shankar," I went over to inform him, "Honestly, it is not a good idea for me to continue today." He looked at me with a searing stare. Suddenly I became concerned that Shankar thought I was some sort of 'faker'. After all, he didn't know me well. Up until now, we had hiked one full day at which point I had told him I was ill, and then two straight days in Jagat I had had to tell him we were staying put. Now we had walked just a few hours and I was laying up again. This bothered me. While I had never been a particularly skilled long-distance hiker, I had always hung in there. "I'm a Calvinist," I liked to joke with people. "I show up every day."

"Bill, we need to go to Dharapani," Shankar said. *We need to go to Dharapani?*

"Yes, I know," I responded defensively. "But honestly, I still have fever. It would be really stupid for me to go any higher this afternoon." Then, in a fit of desperation, I said, "Tomorrow I will be well. We will walk a full day." Of course, that was just a leap of hope.

It was difficult to tell how much Shankar understood me. He returned to talking with the other porters. I was beginning to feel some distance opening up between the two of us. I started wondering if hanging with these other Nepali boys was his main concern. Again he turned to me and said—well, I think he said, but I was not sure—"Bill, I go to Dharapani." *Oh shit. He's going to mutiny. And I've already paid him, so I have no leverage.*

"Shankar," I quickly said. "We have plenty of time." I pulled out the guidebook and virtually promised that we would follow a particular schedule that would get him to the finish by the expiration of his contract on the 16th day.

"Yes," he said, while looking at the ground.

I'm sitting here defensively explaining myself to a porter. Damn, damn.

I immediately went looking for a teahouse where I could put two beds together. That wasn't tough to find with everybody blowing town. Tal easily had over 100 beds; yet no more than ten people had chosen to stay. These Gurung cowboys may be the most rugged people I ever saw. But there was an air of glumness that hung over the empty town, as trekker after trekker pulled themselves up from the lunch table and packed up to leave.

***

What the hell is this? It can't be rain. The monsoon season is supposed to end in September.

I was taking an afternoon siesta, but kept hearing something beating heavily against the metal roof of the teahouse. Finally, I looked out the window where a stooped elderly lady was hauling heavy loads of wash around. And sure enough, it was pouring rain. *I made the right decision.* Cold rain pelting me right now at a higher elevation would probably have had me in a state of great paranoia.

When the rain ended at dark, I went wandering around the dirt road of the virtually empty town, vainly hoping to see a familiar face. But all I saw was more stray animals. So I returned to the teahouse to order dinner. Morale was downbeat tonight. Young couples like the one who owned this teahouse habitually put every resource at their command into starting up such a venture. But tonight I was the only customer.

The owner's sister, who looked to be no more than 22 or 23, was put in charge of serving me. She was a chunky girl with an obvious Mongolian ancestry. And let me just say – these people don't just look tough; they live tough. In fact, it was widely remarked upon that the women seemed to work even harder than the men. Everywhere you looked, females of all ages were toiling diligently, whether it be fetching and burning wood, cooking, cleaning, and, of course, raising kids. But I was lonely tonight and wanted to chat. So did this young lady in a very direct style.

"Do you have a boyfriend?" I asked her.

"No, no boys in this town?"

"Are you looking for a boyfriend?" I asked her.

"Yes."

"Do you like tall or short guys?"

"Tall," she answered. "Can you get me job in America?"

"Yes, but you will have to marry an American first."

"You married?"

"Never."

"You marry me?" she asked me. Obviously this conversation was speculative BS; or at least I assume it was.

"Yes," I accepted her marriage proposal. "And the honeymoon is tonight." The rugged, even primitive lifestyles in these hinterlands should be respected. But it should not be over-romanticized. This young lady seemed very results-oriented. She probably wasn't fulfilled here in this provincial town and might like to live a little bit.

"How old you?" she asked me. *Oops. Does she really have to know?*

"I prefer questions about my height," I answered, which was only a half-lie, and tried to move on to another topic. But my filibuster didn't work.

"How old you?" she again asked, looking me in the eyes.

"51," I answered her straight back.

"You 51," she confirmed.

"Yes," I stared straight at her, in a feeble attempt to go on a counter-offensive.

"No," she said. Nothing else.

All flirtation and extraneous conversation immediately ceased. Nonetheless, I didn't regret our brief 'fling' one bit. At least 'the high drama' got my mind off my health obsession for a brief moment.

CHAPTER 8

Getting in the Game

Yes, I wanted part of the action on the Annapurna Circuit. But no, I was not brooding over last night's foul ball. It had mostly been *pro-forma* anyway. Honestly.

In stark terms, it was simply too damn cold anyway in these teahouses for an icicle like myself to even contemplate any such 'congress' with anyone. I knew deep in marrow that I was not well cut out for high elevations and cold weather. It was critical to stay focused. Fortunately, the night in Tal proved to be a success in this regard. Bundled up heavily in my sleeping bag and wearing long johns and an Icelandic sweater, I had slept deeply and awoken feeling better.

However, a perverse juxtaposition had taken hold in my relationship with my porter. I honestly felt like I now needed to prove my *bona-fides* to Shankar by walking a full day. It was a 6-hour walk to *Danagyu*, with 1,800 feet (550 meters) of elevation gain. I felt like I had to make it there today.

The scenery leaving Tal quickly became dramatic. Another spectacular waterfall was rushing off the hillside. Rarely was it possible to tell where these cascades originated; about all you knew was that solid glaciers lay way, way up above us down here at 6,000

Ledge walking is an integral feature of the Annapurna Circuit

feet. However, my giddiness quickly waned as the wide valley of Tal narrowed to the point that we were suddenly staring directly at a falloff of hundreds of feet into the gorge on our left. Meanwhile, the rock walls on our right descended to the point that anybody over two meters tall found themselves choosing between having to duck under them or edge close to the precipice on the left. Fortunately the resourceful *Anna Purna Conservation Area Project* (ACAP,) had constructed metal rails to prevent a tragic fall. I hurried forward with my head down.

My grim mood didn't let up any when we came across another of the suspension bridges leading back over to the west side of the river. I fully admit they these bridges just weren't that difficult to cross; but you did have to completely adjust your stride and – in my case – dig into as deep a crouch as possible. This time I waited for Shankar to fully cross to not impede my stability.

Once across, we passed a tall, thin young lady with long, black hair, who seemed to be wearing some trekker version of fashion clothing. But the most startling thing about her was her eyes – dark, bewitching eyes. I would soon learn she was Israeli. No surprise there. Israelis seem to alternate between American-style transparency and Chinese-style inscrutability. I normally break into conversation with just about any stray trekker. But I still was looking to get my stride and continued on ascending as the morning sun roasted us.

Finally Shankar and I arrived in the village of Dharapani, which had originally been yesterday's destination. *I would have had trouble sleeping up here.* But that thought was fundamentally incoherent for the simple reason that this would be the veritable lowlands in a few days.

"I need a break," I announced to Shankar and moved over to the shade. For the second day in a row, a dark look came over Shankar. Without responding he went over to chat with some Nepali boys. *Does he have some agenda I don't know about?* He always made me feel uncomfortable about taking breaks. My number one concern was to not get any more fever. That meant taking some more Iburprofen and pouring down a full liter of water. After a half-hour I said, "Shankar, are you ready?" Without really even acknowledging me, he came back over, picked up my backpack and we headed out of town. At the village's edge, we came upon two security checkpoints.

"Permits," Shankar said.

Like most people, security and document stations in foreign countries tend to put me in a low-level state of worry. In Latin America I had been forced to bribe some pretty awful-looking humanoids to gain entry and exit at various places. But I would soon see that here in Nepal, my concerns were unfounded.

The second permit we were required to have was the TMS—

Trekking Management System, which was intended to keep track of our whereabouts. There were a few sinister suggestions that this served Maoist purposes to monitor us so closely. But the truth is almost surely less malevolent. There is a long history of trekkers getting lost in these mountainous environs. Having these monitoring stations facilitates search and rescue, if somebody does go AWOL.

***

I'm headed a place like I've never been before. That was my predominant emotion as we came upon yet another awesome waterfall crashing down to our right, fed by the Tulagi glacier of the Manaslu range to our east. To our west stood towering snowcapped peaks (we were walking almost due north towards the Tibet-Chinese border). This whole Annapurna Circuit was beginning to seem like a test, in colloquial terms, mostly about 'keeping one's shit together'.

Ever upward we trekkers go

I continued having to take more breaks than I was accustomed to. But as the cooler afternoon temperatures prevailed they became shorter. By mid-afternoon, we ascended up a steep forested slope into the village of *Danagyu*. It seemed pretty typical – a lone dirt street with scattered animals and lined with teahouses. One nice touch was that the *ACAP* had constructed a water station here. So instead of having to pay extortionate prices for bottled water, I could buy treated water at a reasonable price.

In Kathmandu a bottle of water had cost 20 rupees (25 cents). In Jagat it was 50 rupees. Now the price in the local commissary was 80 rupees.

***

Despite having finally put in a full day, my mood was downbeat. Up until now, the temperatures had at least been moderate throughout the daytime hours, before the nighttime chill. But now, a cool, whipping wind had forced me to bundle up earlier. *What's it going to be like up there?*

Again, I dropped my backpack at Shankar's feet and commenced racing around the village, randomly popping in bedrooms with teahouse owners standing by looking confused. Finally I found one up towards the top of the hill that fit my needs. But besides being abandoned, it seemed almost spooky. For that reason, once I had everything orchestrated in my room, I went out to the patio which overlooked the main street, hoping to maybe convince some other trekkers to stay here.

Two very athletic-looking ladies that I had not seen before came loping confidently up the main street. "*Namaste*," I said, employing the catch-all Nepalese salutation. This was especially useful for trekkers on Annapurna Circuit for the simple reason that you rarely knew what nationality anybody was at first glance.

"*Namaste*," they both replied. Fortunately (for me, anyway), the *lingua franca* on the Annapurna Circuit is English. Everybody from the French, to the Israelis, the Germans, the Chinese, the porters and guides all strive to communicate in English.

"Where did you stay last night?" I asked the two ladies who

appeared to be in their thirties.

"Ghermu," the shorter, more solid one, answered.

"I should have known," I replied. They had started the day several kilometers behind and 1,000 feet below where I had begun. "And you must be from Australia."

"Yes, how did you know," the lankier one asked.

"Because of the distance you have gone today." That drew an appreciative laugh from them and I added it on thick. "And it explains why you are so easy to chat with."

It's easy to sing the Aussies praises for a simple reason – they are so damn nice. Of course, why in the world wouldn't you have a sunny disposition if you lived in a place with so much land and sunshine.

"There are lots of empty rooms here," I said. A short discussion ensued between them, in which I heard the shorter one say the name, "Harold Holt." Harold Holt, of course, was the Australian Prime Minister who was paddling in the shallow waters of the ocean in 1967 when a sudden riptide helplessly swept him away. The largest search and rescue operation in Australian history commenced, but never yielded the slightest clue. However, rather than be embarrassed by what happened their Prime Minister, Australians have learned to make light of it. There is commonly used Australian salutation, "doing the Harold Holt bolt," which means to get the hell out of some place right away.

These girls decided to do the Harold Holt bolt straight out of town. My nagging sense of inferiority again flared up, as they traipsed on up the main dirt road, passing by a couple stray cows on their way out of the village to higher elevations.

CHAPTER 9

Nepalese Pride

"The geography of the country is a ten," I opined. "The people are a ten. The food is a *seven* in these teahouses."

"No," a native-sounding voice sharply interrupted me, "everything up here is a ten." I turned and looked into the mountain-weathered face of a middle-aged Nepali man. He didn't actually look angry. Nor did he appear especially indignant. But he did come off as intensely 'invested' in the situation. And he had spoken up.

The man was the porter for a group of Israelis I had walked much of the day with. We were all huddled together in the dining room of a teahouse in the village of *Chame*. Most of the teahouses had signs announcing '24 hour hot showers'. But in reality, things like hot showers were for those few irritating trekkers who insisted on not taking breaks and racing so that they could use up the hot water. Our options were narrowing, the higher up we went. The bedrooms of the teahouses were cold and drafty—suitable only for wrapping oneself up to go to bed. The best bet for staying warm was the wooden stoves here in the teahouse dining rooms. We had now entered the stage where trekkers hovered around these for three or four hours each evening. Moods were palpably gloomier.

Amongst this group was the dark headed girl with the even darker eyes we had passed after crossing the suspension bridge out of Tal. Bar was her name. To no great surprise, Bar was telling me that she had just finished her two year service requirement in the Israeli military.

"I was an officer," she had added.

"Well then, Annapurna is a piece of cake for you."

"No," she had stated matter-of-factly, "it's not. But I wanted something different after the military."

"Well, couldn't you have found something more relaxing than this?" I had countered. But I have seen Israelis all over the place in my own far-flung peregrinations. Sedentary vacations just are not their cup of tea. So it was no big surprise they were so well represented on Annapurna.

Tonight's discussion had been virtually monopolized by the increasingly critical subject of altitude pills. Most everybody was carrying them (*Diamox*), and some had already begun taking doses. However, others were vowing that they weren't going to take them at all. "No, I should think not," one Englishman drolly noted. "They dehydrate you *and* make you pee at the same time."

Then there was a third group that had not begun taking them, but was worried they should be doing so. That latter group included myself. "I hear it is *not* smart to *not* take them," one Israeli man said in some carefully hedged logic that actually made sense to me. But the fact was that you could expect altitude pills to bring on symptoms, including dizziness; so it was all a delicate dance.

The specific concern I had was that my medicine bottle contained a warning to not take aspirin together with Diamox. However, I had been regularly taking Ibuprofen since I had taken ill. Throughout the night the Israelis had been calling a doctor back home with various questions about their own altitude pills.

Finally, I had asked Bar's father, "Hey, is there any way you can ask the doctor whether I can take Advil (ibuprofen) with the Diamox?"

His shoulders had slumped. "The doctor is on vacation," he had explained. "We've already called him three times tonight." But then he had reconsidered and gone outside to call a fourth time. Soon he had come back in with the news that I had a green light to go ahead and begin my Diamox prescription in tandem with the Advil. The big mountain pass lay just five days, but more than 9,000 feet in elevation above us.

Once we had gotten those vital matters taken care of, we had turned to the critical subject of food. That is when I had made my sweeping judgment of Nepalese geography, people, and cuisine. The room had abruptly gone silent with this Nepali porter's challenge of my remark.

"Hey," I tried to recover, "a seven out of ten for the food is very good for being way up here in the mountains." Then I turned to the Israelis and said, "Don't you agree that a seven is good considering the conditions?" But they stayed mum and let me fight this one out myself. After all, it was their porter that I was debating.

"But you must remember," the porter bore in, "that food has to be carried up these mountains by animals. My first job in the mountains when I was 13 was doing food transport." *That* kicked my inferiority complex back up.

"Yes, yes," I agreed. "But I still say that a seven is good for the mountains." Of course it was all an esoteric subject, the kind of thing you talk about when you have too much time on your hands, which we did. But the food was not only getting more expensive the higher we got (very understandable, and still reasonably priced by Western standards), but less ample. And the soup was turning noticeably more watery each night.

But putting it all in perspective, the food was still a helluva' lot better than the awful hiker food that we ate on the Appalachian and Pacific Crest Trails. So maybe I should learn to follow the Israeli example and just shut up.

CHAPTER 10

The Mountains

The best time to hike in the Himalayas is early in the morning. The cool, moist air burns up the minute the bright yellow sun clears the banks of the towering peaks to our east. You can expect to be shedding one layer of clothing after another. And if you are health conscious, this may be the only chance to inhale ample quantities of *Vitamin D*, otherwise so difficult to get here up in the mountains.

But there was another more daunting pattern—the higher up, the less time the sunshine lasted. By the time we had finally cleared 10,000 feet on the way to Pisang, the sunshine would give way to cool, windswept, overcast conditions by 10:00 in the morning. It was a delight to trek in, but you could expect to promptly be adding back layers of clothing.

I remembered the first time in my life above 10,000 feet in the Sierra Nevada Mountains on the Pacific Crest Trail. "It looks so normal," I kept exclaiming. "It's almost surreal to think how high we are." This Himalayan scene also looked normal at times; but it also had an increasingly isolated feel to it. For starters, the rushing water down below was crashing along the rocks of the gorge with an ever-great thrust, the closer we got to its mountain source. And then there was the fact that we just kept walking in the direction of these enormous cathedral-like peaks.

"You see that mountain right there," Shankar said, pointing southeast to a gargantuan peak. "That is *Manaslu*." I turned and stared directly at the eighth highest mountain in the

Trekkers routinely stare directly on world-class peaks

world (26,759 feet). It appeared to be just a few miles from where we now stood; but given its monstrosity, it was probably further. Strangely enough, there was something about taking it in here in full that was both intimidating and comforting. Most of what we were staring at was a mass of sandstone and granite, but with a brilliant snow-capped peak gleaming in the sun. I kept trying to figure out where 17,800 feet (the height of Thorung La Pass) would be on this mountain.

"Do you think there is snow at the top of Thorung La Pass?" I asked Shankar for the third or fourth time since meeting him.

"No," he shook his head. "No snow." That was encouraging. However, I needed constant wet nursing and kept staring at Manaslu.

"That snow right there on Manaslu," I continued pressing Shankar, "does it begin at a higher elevation than Thorung La Pass?" Shankar stared at Manaslu for a good while and then said, "Yes, higher." *I should be able to make it over Thorung La Pass.*

Shankar and I turned a corner and saw two young women

standing in the middle of the trail chatting in English.

"Are you from England?" I predictably asked.

"Do we seem that unfriendly?" the younger one responded. Good line, even if it's true. Actually, they were not English, but from Scotland (one had grown up in Wales). Rhona and Bronwen were their names and they lived in Edinborough and Glasgow.

"Well you've got an advantage, right?" I asked.

"Why?"

"Isn't this just like the Scottish Highlands?"

"Minus the oxygen," Bronwen responded.

It was good to see some women hiking together. On the Appalachian Trail and El Camino de Santiago, both of which are trails of the masses, women routinely head out together with other women; many even set off alone. But I had seen very little of that on the Annapurna Circuit. And you couldn't really blame them either; these mountains do have a forbidding quality to them.

***

Speaking of groups of women, Annapurna was the scene of one of the most storied female expeditions of all time. In the late 1970's, Arlene Blum, an American mountaineer, set her periscope on becoming the first woman to ascend Annapurna I, the tenth highest peak in the world.

Most people would agree the bravery of her decision greatly exceeded its wisdom. As of her attempt in 1978, seventeen different individuals had attempted to summit Annapurna. Eight of them had actually summited, while nine had died. Nonetheless, Blum was able to put together a party of nine American women and one British lady. To finance the journey they raised $80,000 through sales of 15,000 T-shirts bearing the slogan, '*A Woman's Place is on Top—Annapurna*'.

From the outset, Blum made it clear that the expedition team was undertaking this dangerous mission on behalf of women the world over. For that reason, they were almost fanatically determined to place at least some of the women on the summit and in the record books.

However, *Old Lady Luck* was showing her capricious nature in the fall of 1978. The party had braved violent winds and mammoth avalanches to push to within 800 feet of the summit. But suddenly they heard a great cloud of snow and ice coming down from the right side of the Sickle. It looked as though three members of her team were directly in its path. Miraculously they were able to scurry a few feet ahead before the blast arrived. It was now time for the leader, Blum, to make tough decisions. As recounted in her gripping narrative, *Annapurna—A Woman's Place*, the following dialogue ensued between the women:

> Blum: "Things that aren't supposed to happen are happening twice a day right now. I feel as if something is telling us we should give up before one of us dies."
>
> *Long silence*
>
> Whitehouse: "I don't feel like talking about it. I just want to climb this mountain."
>
> Miller: I've been climbing for twenty years and I've never been on a mountain so unstable. The avalanches are completely random. Sometimes it seems almost immoral to keep going."

The decision fell to the leader, Arlene Blum. 'The avalanche danger was so great that we seriously had to consider giving up," she wrote. "But the momentum of the ascent overwhelmed our doubts and the climbing continued." A party of two women and two Sherpas groped their way to the top to make history.

"We weren't actually trying to act heroic – everyone was bitching and saying they were afraid," Blum later wrote. "I'm not sure it was particularly intelligent or laudable for us to continue. But it definitely was heroic." *That*, in a nutshell, is the history of high altitude mountaineering.

Alas, a second party of two women, Vera Watson and Allison Chadwick, were determined to summit themselves. This was unusual for the simple reason that momentum normally wanes after the first team summits. Worse yet, the two Sherpas felt like they were getting High Altitude Mountain Sickness themselves, and refused to ascend with the second party of women. Nonetheless, this second party continued up, without any Sherpa support, to within a few hundred feet of the top. However—either because of steep ice or a rock fall—they fell 1,500 feet to their deaths. An attempt to recover the bodies of the two ladies was quickly abandoned as too dangerous.

When the tragic reality finally became clear, the other eight ladies locked arms and sang the old Quaker song, 'Tis the gift to be simple, 'tis the gift to be free…"

Despite its tragic implications, this mission, which took place about 20 miles (30 kilometers) to the east of where we now stood, had rightfully earned its place in the annals.

***

The two Scottish girls were afflicted with no such obsessions. In fact, their cool, offhanded ways were the perfect ethos for the Annapurna Circuit itself. Indeed, their style proved to be understated. After we did the steep climb up into the village of

Pisang, where everybody was staying the evening, the two girls asked, "Would you like to have a look at *Upper Pisang*?" It was another thousand foot climb over completely exposed terrain.

"You're not going right this minute are you?" I asked.

"Yes, I reckon we'll have a go at it," Rhona said softly. Off they went.

Normally I would find myself passing the two of them a couple times a day; yet they often ended the day up ahead of me. But being an admirer of flexible traveling, this did not bruise my male ego one bit. Rather, my morale was hanging in there, as my health and strength had improved. I was in about as good of shape as a middle-aged person of average abilities, who also happens to hate being cold, can expect to be in above 10,000 feet. Perhaps even better yet, I was also becoming an admirer of the Annapurna Circuit, itself.

Whether it was farsighted trail designers or the luck of nature, the Circuit seemed a good fit for a person like me. In and of itself, it was not that difficult. This was especially impressive considering we were winding through and around some of the world's greatest peaks. But when you throw in the cold nighttime weather and ever-thinning air, it becomes a much stiffer challenge. Up until now, it had not proven to be too terribly difficult. Our daily ascent was about 1,300 to 1,400 feet on average, which usually took about six hours to cover. However, given my past debilities in cold weather and high elevation, I knew to not be overly confident.

I also was aware that once we got to Manang we would be entering an entirely different phase of the trek—one that would be more challenging and, yes, more dangerous. That's when it would all boil down to that one word, 'acclimatization'.

CHAPTER 11

Acclimatization

"Are we sure to get a place in Manang?" I asked Shankar.

"Yes," Shankar answered.

Manang. From the very beginning, everyone had been talking about the pivotal role this village played in the Annapurna Circuit. This was where we had universally been advised to take an acclimatization day at just above 11,000 feet (3,540 meters), before the pace of altitude gain would accelerate. Of course, that meant having to spend two nights there. And since everybody else was doing the same, the demand for teahouse rooms would presumably be double that of every other village.

"Are there double the number of teahouses in Manang of all the other villages?" I asked him. It wasn't clear he understood my point. Perhaps the reason that the Nepalis are such agreeable folks is that they are so endearingly unsophisticated about such business concepts as supply and demand. A person growing up in a country this poor and rugged knows from the outset that life is going to be demanding. They expect to work hard their entire lives; for that reason you don't feel like they are trying to constantly outsmart you.

Shankar just nodded his head at my question and said, "Yes, hotels." However, the guides of some other trekkers were painting a more complex story. Many of them had either booked rooms in advance or were calling ahead. Others touted their connections in one or another teahouse. But Shankar and I were completely on a shoestring. For that reason we were cutting the breaks short. Finally, in the early afternoon we cleared a hilltop where a remote mountain outpost came into view. Shankar had told me Manang was the biggest village on the Circuit. But to the naked eye, it didn't appear even as large as Chame, where we had stayed a couple nights before.

Yak cows – one of the many symbols of the highlands

Just before entering town, Shankar pointed at some bulky, especially shaggy animals with large horns, "Those, Bill. Yak cow." *How could anyone kill something so docile looking?*

However, once we entered the traditional gateway to the city, the first thing I saw was a restaurant offering 'Yak Burgers'. *Hmmm.* My meat diet, like most trekkers, had been deficient up to this point; I was losing weight. Thus, I had no problem altering my prior point of view. Better yet, the two Australian girls who had done the 'Harold Holt Bolt' out of Danagyu were sitting there having a Yak Burger out on the terrace.

"Hello, Harold Holt," I said, generating a knowing laughter. "How are those burgers?"

"Delicious," the fair-headed one said. "Feel free to join us."

"I can't wait," I said. "But I've got to get a room first. Where are you staying?"

"You see that big old building up there on the right."

"Yeah, are there any rooms?"

"Some people left this morning."

"We'll go get a room and come back."

Shankar and I hurried over to the large house they had mentioned. Like most teahouses, it was not obvious who you needed to talk to. Often you would spot a Nepali walking around and ask them if there is a room available, only to find out it was just a porter you were talking to. Here, we made our way inside, where we found a line of people waiting. Word soon came that the teahouse was completely full.

Fortunately, I was at the back of the line which gave me a head start on racing out of the door to other teahouses. Soon we were wandering along a row of teahouses, where we saw lots of familiar faces.

"Are there any rooms available?" I called up to a few trekkers.

"I don't think so," was invariably the response.

It became apparent that we had been outflanked by our colleagues, and I began to get a bit panicky. I needed to stay two nights in this town, but couldn't even find a room for one. Further, the map showed the next town was Gunsang, which was another 1,200 feet higher in elevation. Yeah, I could probably make it there by dark; but that would defeat the whole purpose of acclimatization.

Other trekkers who had been rejected from teahouses joined several large cows in wandering around the village seemingly without purpose. I began doing my customary ricocheting thing. But it wasn't even clear which of the one-floor stone buildings in town actually provided lodging. Finally I spotted a lodge that had some nice-looking wooden cottages out back. Better yet, rather than being holed up in a cool, grungy room of brick and stone, I would be 'protected' by wood and glass.

At dinner that evening, I chatted with a Russian guy who seemed very at ease. As we chatted he poured cup after cup of mint tea. "Mint tea puts you to sleep," he said plainly. I tried some. Indeed, it put me to sleep for a good hour. But then I spent the rest of the night adding layer after layer of clothing, seven layers in all, but with little comfort gained. The wood and glass cottages proved to be no match for the uglier stone hovels trekkers habitually bivouack in.

When I told the Russian guy about it in the morning, he said, "No Bill, the insulation of your sleeping bag is what keeps you warm. If you wear too many clothes, it will make you less warm." *Damn blunder*. And given that he was Russian, he probably knew what he was talking about concerning cold.

At first light, I began barging into teahouses aggressively asking for a room for the day. Finally, one said I could return at 10:00 for a room. I went and sat sullenly in the early-morning sun, which was the one time all day that you could really count on being warm. I savored it.

A British couple that I had met back at the teahouse in Jagat came by on their way out of town after a day of acclimatization. They were an unusually healthy-looking, congenial pair. But today they had a different look in their faces.

"I'm more worried about the cold than the altitude," the girl said. Her face had a seriousness of purpose that it had lacked before as she stared off up into the rugged mountains where we were all headed.

***

The focal point of an acclimatization day in Manang is at 3:00 in the afternoon. This is when the masses of trekkers in the village head to the Medical Aid Center of the *Himalayan Rescue Association* (HRA) for the daily acclimatization briefing. It wasn't actually mandatory, but might as well have been. Even before leaving for Nepal, I had read about the need to attend this presentation. And all along the way there had been much talk about it.

The building was packed to standing room. The Association had been established in 1973 to educate trekkers about the deadly threat of altitude sickness after several members of a Japanese expedition had suddenly dropped dead. Indeed, statistics show they have been very successful. Deaths in this area from altitude sickness, which had averaged in double digits annually for decades, now are down to less than a handful per year despite a sharp increase in the number of trekkers.

Actually, volunteering to work for the HRA is considered a prestige position because of the unique experience in the Himalayas. A Swiss French physician who spoke thickly accented English took to the podium.

"The symptoms of high altitude mountain sickness are a headache, nausea, fatigue, dizziness, or sleep disturbance," she said. "How many of you have experienced any of these symptoms?" Only about 50% of trekkers raised their hands. That came as a surprise to me. For I had already experienced every single one of them.

I raised my hand and asked her about altitude pills.

"You should take one-half pill (Diamox) in the morning and another half in the evening," she answered.

"But when I take them I get a sharp tingling sensation in my hands," someone noted.

"This is why you must drink at least four liters of water per day at this elevation. To help your body deal with all these symptoms." Sounded reasonable. However, it was worth noting that there would be no more bottles of water for sale after Manang. Rather, we were to buy the water from the drinking stations in the village. *What will be the price of water up there?*

"The most important way to acclimatize," she said in closing, "is to climb at least 500 feet higher than where you are going to sleep, and then descend back down." In climber's parlance, this is known as *climb high, sleep low.* Many trekkers would prove to be good pupils in this regard; I had seen people climbing all over of the mountains around Manang. And after enjoying every bite of a yak burger, I scaled most of the way up a nearby mountain, although truth be known as much to keep my body temperature up as for acclimatization.

When I finally got back to my room, I decided that tonight was my last best hope for getting a good night's sleep before the big summit day over Thorung La Pass, coming up in three days. But both beds had footboards on all sides, which made it impossible to marry them seamlessly together. My years of experience told me to just forget the bed frames and throw both mattresses on the floor. However there wasn't enough room on the floor for both of them. I thrashed and strained moving things things around, before finally placing one bed frame on top of the other. This gave me the extra room I needed to put the mattresses in a T-format. I then lay down on my extra-long floor bed and got my best night's sleep on the Annapurna Circuit. When I woke up in the morning I was actually proud of myself for such adaptability!

And thus it was that I was able to head off well rested on a three day ascent to the Pass, the likes of which are available very few places in the world.

CHAPTER 12

The High Leagues

Ambience. That's what dominated my mind on the way out of Manang to the highest elevations I ever have been, or probably ever will go. Everything just seemed different. The last traces of green vanished at about 12,000 feet, as we marched steadily up the modestly inclined Annapurna Circuit. A biting wind whistling down from the upper mountains held the temperature in check.

Strangely enough though, as profoundly vast as everything was, it nonetheless seemed confining in some ways. The so-called 'High Sierra' in central California features yawning vistas that seemingly go on into infinity. But here, steep walls of rock and granite rose up at virtually ninety degree angles. However, after ascending further, we would find ourselves enveloped in an enormous valley with ridges blocking our view of the towering peaks. But then we would ascend some more and soon would be staring at the Annapurna range again in its entirety.

And nobody was taking breaks. That bothered me. But it must be said that for the first time I, too, was guilty of racing. Once again I was asking Shankar, "Are there many lodges in *Yak Kharka*?" But he continued giving me vague answers. So we walked non-stop at a brisk pace. Incidentally, that is specifically what the doctor yesterday ordered us not to do. "You must not hurry at high elevations," the doctor had exhorted us. "It is dangerous."

By now we were accustomed to stepping aside the trail a few times a day to allow herds of horses and donkeys to clod by, with their packs either bulging or empty. But that was no longer the case, as the terrain had become too dangerous for pack animals to traverse. Instead, human porters hauling large baskets of essential goods marched with their heads facing straight down at the ground, carrying what was, in effect, our lifeline. Expecting the worst in terms of prices, I had bought more food and water than normal in Manang to ease the financial blow up ahead.

I stood over to the side as a caravan of human porters came steaming by. One thing I liked about these porters was their self-esteem. Let's face it – in Third World Countries, Lesser Developed Countries, whatever you want to call them – the local people often play second fiddle to us pampered foreign tourists. But anybody and everybody could see that the people working the hardest, making the most valuable contributions, and showing the most courage, were the porters. On narrow passages of the trail, they would come barreling down the center of the trail; it was up to us to stand aside.

A big Australian girl was also standing there waiting on the porters to pass by. Her name was Kate. I had seen her on several occasions and, like most Australians, she had a perennially sunny personality. Adding to her sense of wonderment was that this was Kate's first time ever outside of her home country. She was habitually one of the first trekkers out each morning, and maintained a very modest pace. Her porter sometimes called ahead to get a reservation.

"Did your porter call ahead, Kate?" I asked, hoping the answer would be 'no'.

"Yes," she said, "but they are not taking reservations in Yak Kharka."

"What do you do if they aren't any rooms up there?"

"We shall see," Kate answered cheerfully, as Shankar and I hurried on for selfish reasons.

On the way up we even passed a lady riding a horse.

"No fair," I said.

"Oh, yeah it is," she answered skeptically in an indeterminate European accent. Indeed, the horse was pitching back and forth, as it went about trying to mount a couple jagged rocks in its way. *I'm glad I'm not on that horse.*

Shankar and I arrived at *Yak Kharka*, meaning 'pasture of the yak cows' at 12:00. This was the earliest we had ever arrived in a village to stay for the evening, which was a dubious feat. We rushed inside where I was told they had one wooden and glass cottage empty in the back. I took a look, and it immediately reminded me of the poorly insulated cottage back in Manang. But I had no other option.

Kate arrived later than me, only to be told there was absolutely nothing available. "Well I'll just have to eat lunch and go on, won't I," she said.

Truth be told, I felt a bit small.

***

The big problem with getting to your destination so early is your body temperature ebbs the rest of the day. I sat there glumly chatting with Kate over lunch, hoping her buoyant nature would perk me up. When she finished her lunch, she stood up and said, "Well, I had better be going now."

But there were no Harold Holt jokes about bolting; she

absolutely had to find a place in the tiny village up ahead (fortunately she did). And I was to feel even guiltier thirty minutes later when an experienced porter told me, "Those cottages where you stay—I have many clients complain." I immediately walked down and asked the owner if I could sleep in the dining hall, which he agreed to. Had I known earlier, Kate could have had the room.

Meanwhile, all the trekkers poured into the main dining hall, where a long afternoon of waiting commenced. This was one of those situations in which it was impossible to tell just how worried everybody was. Perhaps that was because there was a large party of British trekkers staying at the teahouse. I told my obligatory joke: 'Is it true that you Englishman are now putting Viagra in the toothpaste in order to maintain stiff upper lips?' That drew the desired chuckles from the members of that doughty island race. But in the middle of it, we suddenly heard a helicopter nearing and preparing to land. "What do we have here?" an older chap named Roger asked. Everybody else sat there in silence. But surely we were all thinking the same thing. *Altitude Mountain Sickness. Evacuation.*

When the helicopter landed in a small field down from the teahouse I ran outside and joined a big crowd of onlookers. Somebody was lying on a stretcher, but I couldn't tell who. With impressive dispatch, the Himalayan Rescue Association strapped the person onto the stretcher and loaded him or her up. They hopped in themselves, lifted up with dispatch, and were gone. *Wow, they are good at that.*

"Who was that?" I asked around. But nobody knew. When I went back inside the dining hall, even the perennially reserved British were pesky about trying to find out what had happened. As it was, everybody just sat there, although the atmosphere now had a slightly eerie undertone. *We're up here. Just about anybody's number could be called.* As it so happened, though, the person evacuated was the Italian lady who had ridden her horse up here. To be sure, she got very professional service. However, from the stories I heard, the whole misadventure would set her back several thousand dollars for the evacuation. In fact, the Himalayan Rescue Association now requires evacuees to sign a payment guarantee before liftoff.

Per my basic acclimatization training, I forced myself to climb several hundred more feet up from the teahouse. Ironically, it was while doing this climb in the cold, barren hills above Yak Kharka that I was the most comfortable – and warm – I had been all day. *If I can just get some semblance of a night's sleep, I should be okay.*

Back in the teahouse, all our bodies were collectively able to keep the room temperature tolerable until dark. Of course, up until now that had been the most blissful hour of the entire day when the wooden stoves in the middle of the dining halls were loaded up with wood and fired up. Trekkers had been able to count on sustenance from these two or three hours of toastiness. But slowly, we began to wonder if it was going to happen tonight.

"Are they going to put wood in the stove?" one Englishman asked his guide. But the normally voluble guide just shrugged his shoulders. A German man broke the truth to us. "They do not heat the stoves up here because it is too expensive to bring the wood up."

"Oh yes, why didn't that occur to me," the Englishman responded, tilting his head back. Nobody complained – we all knew we were lucky to be eating.

This also made my plan to sleep in the dining hall dubious. By the time everyone had cleared out to their rooms, the temperature had palpably fallen. The end result was I ended up moving around the room three times during the evening, each ensuing position less comfortable – and less warm – than the previous one.

Of course, I had had my share of nights like this on the Appalachian and Pacific Crest Trails. What I had learned was that, yeah, it was a problem. But you could dig deep for a few days and make up for it. That's where my hopes for a successful summit two days hence now lay. But the pace of acclimatization was only going to accelerate.

***

The scene leaving *Yak Kharka* was the bleakest yet. For the first time there was no morning sunshine at all, but rather a cool, windy, and overcast day. Alpine scrub and large boulders dotted the bleak landscape.

Soon we arrived at a yak pasture teeming with cows, which had everyone reaching for their cameras. The amateur Darwin in me has long since noticed that animals in colder climates do *not* have long limbs or necks that would make it difficult to retain body heat. In the case of humans, Eskimos have adapted over the millennia and have notoriously short limbs and trunks. The British girl's words back in Manang kept reverberating in my mind—"I'm more worried about the cold than the altitude."

Again, everybody was seemingly in a fly pattern, with few people taking the breaks that had been so enjoyable up until Manang. The stark truth was they would have been especially helpful at this elevation in the task of acclimatization. But feeling like I had no choice, I joined in the race. The Circuit itself ascended at modest grades, but also ran along the side of narrow slopes with wicked-looking drop-offs towards the gushing river. Finally, I told Shankar, "Here, short break." I felt a minor shortness of breath, to be sure. But it was nothing alarming.

We sat down on the side of the trail, while trekkers steadily passed by. *Will we be able to get a room?* Person after person had told me, "There is no way they can sell out of rooms in *Thorung Phedi Base Camp*." But they were often the same people who had painted a similar portrait about Manang. Where their forecasts were going astray was in not figuring in these large groups of French, British, and German trekkers who had reserved blocks of rooms months in advance through their trekking agencies. But also, teahouse owners were telling me the number of trekkers on the Circuit this year was up thirty percent. The Annapurna Circuit appears to be a growth industry; all along the way, I was seeing what appeared to be future teahouses being built.

"Do you know what the best lodge is in *Thorung Phedi?*" I asked Shankar. But he remained mum. I had expected a Nepali porter to be enigmatic, to be sure. But this was getting to be a little maddening as we got so close to crunch time. *Has he done the Annapurna Circuit as many times as he claimed he has?* I got restless as familiar faces continued hurrying by. After a few minutes, I said, "Shankar, let's go."

Bleak environs on the trek to Base Camp

When we cleared the crest of a long ridge, my stomach sank at the sight of two long suspension bridges. But as best I could tell, we had a choice. "Which bridge do you recommend?" I asked Shankar. No answer. Most people were headed to the first one. But it actually appeared to be a longer traverse than the second one, which ratcheted up my level of anxiety. Wet and cold is the opportune recipe for hypothermia. We were in an area marked 'Landslide Zone'. All I could think about was going into some uncontrolled slide in the loose dirt before even reaching the suspension bridge. Then the same helicopter as yesterday would be looking for a place to land around here.

"The second bridge looks better," I said to Shankar. "Do you agree?" No answer. But I continued pressing him. "Do you think the second bridge is better?"

"Okay," he said.

Well heck,, technically he was a porter, not a guide. We continued along the ridge where we faced a steep descent in the loose dirt to get to the foot of the bridge. It sure as hell was no surprise this area was marked as a Landslide Zone. *This is not that hard. Keep your cool. And stay the hell away from that water.* For the first time since beginning the Circuit, I removed the modest-sized pack I was carrying, took to my butt, and slid down to the foot of the suspension bridge. "Wait here, Shankar," I motioned and schlepped my way across the last suspension bridge before the pass.

We then commenced another climb in the barren terrain. Again I tried laying down off to the side of the trail; but I simply was not comfortable enough to take a break of any length. Restless, I took to my feet after just a few minutes and continued on.

We came up on another large group marching single-file up the narrow ridge with a steep falloff to our right. Better yet, I soon recognized that this was the large French group that had spent such a jovial evening back in Jagat, while I was holed up ill there. One look at them showed I wasn't the only person daunted by the terrain. The entire group and porters were moving in slow-motion lockstep along what was the narrowest part of the trail. Again, I want to emphasize—this was *not* that hard. But the margin for error was frightful.

Now we could see *Thorung Phedi Base Camp* beckoning in the distance. It always surprised me to see how modestly sized were these places that everybody had been obsessing over for so many days. *I wonder if this big group has reservations.* Once we got past the most precarious part, they all stood to the side and let Shankar and me pass by.

"Oh hello," the lone girl said merrily. "You have obviously gotten well."

"Oh yeah," I said when I realized I was talking to Veronique, the French girl I had met back in Jagat. She appeared to have morphed into the leader of this big group, despite being twenty or thirty years younger than any of the other members. Indeed, that is one of the great things about outdoor journeys – the way sociology often gets completely stood on its head.

"Are you staying here?" Veronique asked.

"If I can find a place. How about you?"

"No, we're going to have lunch and then continue."

"To High Camp?" I asked in amazement.

"Yes," she laughed.

"Damn, I thought about it," I said.

What Veronique was talking about was the *High Base Camp*, which was another 1,450 feet in elevation gain from the Thorung Phedi Base Camp that we were now approaching. In fact, the wisdom of staying at High Base Camp was a hotly debated topic among trekkers. The advantage was obvious. We were facing a

3,200 foot climb (1,000 meters) tomorrow out of Thorung Phedi Base Camp. Further, we had all been advised to begin well before first light in order to get to the summit before the harsh late morning winds that customarily brutalize trekkers at Thorung La Pass. However, if you stayed at High Base Camp it was much easier to get to the Pass before the heavy winds; and your climb was cut by forty percent. What's more, it allows you to acclimatize more fully before reaching 17,768 feet at the Pass.

The downside to sleeping at High Base camp was just as obvious. Some just flat out say it is never a good idea to sleep at such elevations. As much trouble as I had had staying warm last night at Yak Kharka, I was receptive to this message. But further, my guidebook explicitly said that you should never try to make it from Yak Kharka, last night's camp, to High Base Camp in one day ("The night halt at Thorung Phedi Base Camp is a must."). But this French group of predominantly middle-aged males of modest ability was planning to do exactly what was proscribed—they were going to walk all the way up to High Camp today. And Rhona and Bronwen, the two Scottish lasses, had told me last night they were planning to do the same.

"Are you worried about picking up so much elevation in one day?" I had asked them this morning.

"We want to make the climb over the pass shorter," Rhona had responded flatly.

We Americans like to depict these Europeans as effete café cowards. But my experience on the Camino de Santiago – and now the Annapurna Circuit – has been that when the time comes, they know how to get with the program.

CHAPTER 13

Base Camp – Dark Night of the Soul

There was just something about *Thorung Phedi Base Camp*. It had that certain fateful look about it.

As Shankar and I were entering the grounds of the first teahouse, we passed a band of almost a dozen porters lying on the ground, entangled like an octopus. As mentioned before, the porters were not able to carry as many clothes as us trekkers. This scene at my feet looked like a classic coping mechanism that even the most hard bit soul would have found endearing.

"Shankar," I quickly said, "ask if there are any rooms available."

He went inside and spoke with a man, as I watched intently. But the man proceeded to dither for several minutes over some food orders in an inconclusive fashion. But then he handed Shankar a key. We walked down a long row of rooms until we came to a room with two beds; however, a backpack and personal belongings were already strewn over one of them. Soon a post middle-aged man marched in with an alarmed look on his face.

"I want my own room," he stated flatly in an American accent.

"They gave me a key to this room," I explained.

"I want my own room," he repeated.

If I'd felt better I might have mocked him by bellowing *The Star Spangled Banner*. Instead, Shankar and I scurried back in to the restaurant; the man gave us another key and we were soon in an empty room with two beds. *God knows where they put the porters and guides here at Base Camp.* Shankar must have been thinking the same thing because he quietly said, "Bill, me stay here."

"Sure," said.

We were going to have to wake up around 3:30 in the morning anyway to begin the long ascent. Of course, when I say 'wake up', that implies we would be asleep. I was unable to tell how Shankar was sleeping in the cold weather; he was inscrutable in that regard. But I had very low expectations that I would get any sort of decent night's sleep. Long before arriving, ex-Annapurna trekkers had told me, "Well, you don't really sleep up there." Some people probably could pull it off. But at 14,600 feet (4,450 meters), I would be bunking down at an elevation 100 feet higher than the highest place (Mount Whitney) I had ever been. Rather than sleep, my main goal would be to gain enough warmth to relax my body.

I went down where a group of trekkers were having lunch under a sun roof. However, beams of bright light proceeded to bear down on my incipient migraine. The conversation amongst these trekkers was quite spirited. Perversely, however, it served to depress me. *Everybody is coping better than me.* I went and sat down next to the big Australian girl, Kate, who was in her usual high spirits. Her attitude could best be described as 'let-the-chips-fall-where-they-may'.

"What time are you beginning tomorrow?" I asked her.

"My guide says he is going to wake me up at 2:00 and we're to start walking at 3:00."

"Why so damn early?"

"He says it will take me 7 hours to get to the top." *Seven hours.*

I ordered fried spaghetti for lunch, but once again could only pick at it. *Loss of appetite*—a clear symptom.

"Wow, when that sun clears that crest over there," I heard one man say, "it's going to get awful cold here quick." The minute it did happen, the British party of sixteen all got up at once and followed their guide in a 500 foot acclimatization ascent.

Meanwhile, I sat there in a sullen mood, buffered by several layers of clothing, and trying to drink as much water as I could. Yet strangely, I still felt dehydrated. My head had a wobbly sensation, almost like a migraine on steroids. There was absolutely no chance of me taking Advil in the middle of the afternoon and getting rid of this headache as long as I felt dehydrated. Instead I opted for another altitude pill, despite the eerie tingling sensation that would surely follow. *These suckers can't be real healthy. But….*

Finally, I decided to start up the mountain myself. *Hopefully it will improve morale.* It was late afternoon and shadows were lengthening across the mountain. It actually looked more similar to a ski slope than it did to any prior parts of the Annapurna Circuit. We had been hemmed in by sharp, steep mountains on both sides almost the whole way; but now we would actually be going up the face of one.

I quickly felt better as I began to ascend. In fact, after reaching the large rock I had chosen as my objective, I rested a little bit and then decided to ascend some more. After being miserable all day, it was practically exhilarating. Alas, my improved morale lasted only until I got back down to Base Camp, at which point my headache quickly recommenced. I tried doing some more stretching exercises and then decided it was a necessary evil to attempt eating again.

The lodge was packed. But it was not warm and toasty for the same reason as Yak Kharka—prohibitive to get fire wood up this far. Despite seeing all kinds of people I knew, I had no interest in chatting. This was a bad sign given my garrulous nature. Truth be known, I was almost to the point where I was *sick and tired of myself.*

I decided to order what were presumably the two most neutral items on the menu – soup and rice, along with another expensive bottle of water. I was able to take the liquids; but again I barely made a dent in the rice.

***

Do something. Anything. I got up and walked outside, where I began methodically doing some windmills and stretching exercises. It was a good way to clear the mind and at least start off the night in my room warm. The stars always hit me on these evening outings in the Himalayas like at a trip to the planetarium. Tonight, however, there were no stars. But the arctic-like air was actually feasty.

To my complete surprise — and perhaps it sounds foolish to be surprised way up here in the Himalayas — snow flurries began swirling around. *These should be short-lived — probably something to do with the wind and cold.* A few trekkers emerged from the dining room and muttered wry remarks about the snow. But the weather had been so picture perfect day after day, that maybe we had begun to feel good weather was an entitlement. Yes, entitlement. Golly, I had questioned veteran trekkers, to the point of virtual interrogation, and received repeated assurances that there was, in fact, no snow on *Thorung La Pass.* And the truth was that I had an acute interest in the subject of snow on this particular pass, going back a few months.

My mind went back to Atlanta, Georgia at the large *REI* store there. REI, of course, is a mecca for outdoor enthusiasts. I was no different. In fact, it was the single retail outlet in the whole world that I actually enjoyed the shopping experience, mainly due to the expertise of their staff.

"You may or may not need boots on Annapurna," the attendant had told me. "But you will definitely need waterproof shoes."

"But I wore non-waterproof trail shoes on both the Appalachian and Pacific Crest Trails," I had protested.

"Trust me on this," he had said with a knowing look on his face. Actually, it was more of a know-it-all look — the kind we have all seen on countless occasions. But in this case, he really did seem knowledgeable and well meaning. "I'm telling you," he continued, "I've got two friends over there on that Circuit right now. You're asking for trouble not wearing waterproof shoes."

However, later that day, another manager at REI had confidently said, "I wouldn't hesitate to wear low-cut, non-waterproof shoes." But then he, too, had begun backtracking; by the end of the discussion he had me over looking at gators and shoe covers.

On El Camino de Santiago I had watched pilgrims prostrate themselves in the hot, dusty Spanish landscape with heavy boots, and had gingerly advised several of them that it was imperative to change to light, breathable, trail-running shoes. But now here I was in the Himalayas amongst the same crowd of predominantly Europeans, all of whom were wearing boots. At the very least, they had looked more appropriate up here in these mountains. And now it had begun snowing. In fact, it began to pick up and accumulate; I was chased inside our drafty room where I embedded myself for a long evening.

"We wake up at 3:00," Shankar said when he walked into the room.

"No, 4:00," I said. "Do not worry. I will be awake."

Then, despite my utter fear of any and all pills, I threw down four Advil tablets to kill my migraine and chased them with a Diamox altitude pill. *This is the most important night's sleep ever for me. I have to get enough to get rid of this migraine or I simply cannot go forward.*

***

I slept lustily. All the 'chemicals' I had thrown down my throat had 'worked'. Perhaps exhaustion and a migraine can be your ally.

At midnight I woke up no longer feeling a headache, which immediately sent jolts of adrenaline through my body. *Yeah, I'm gonna' go over the Pass today.* But I needed to go the bathroom.

When I bundled up and headed outside to the bathroom, I had not walked five steps before my coat was almost fully pasted with heavy flakes of snow. It was necessary to tread very carefully on the new blanket of snow that carpeted the pavement. Often at night I had simply ventured away from the teahouses to urinate. But with this much snow on the ground, I stuck with the bathroom drain, and the requisite contortions required for my 83 inch (2.12 meter) body under a 68 inch (1.90 meter) roof. When I was returning to my room I looked up at the spotlights which illuminated not just a heavy downfall of snow, but snow-covered hills. *Damn, damn.*

I went back in the room and lay back down on my floor mattress, seemingly attempting to will myself into losing consciousness. But what I experienced instead was a few dark hours of the soul.

I desperately want to get over today. The Pass is only five miles from where I am right this minute. If I can just get there, I can handle the huge descent. Every single step, I will be breathing better and getting warmer.

My mind went back to the Pacific Crest Trail in the American West, where I had contracted a horrible migraine while ascending Mount Whitney. In preparing for Annapurna, I had identified two things that had made the ascent up Whitney worse than it had to be. First, I had shivered in my tent throughout the four nights before the ascent; that had weakened me considerably. And secondly, I had been virtually force-marched up Whitney by a 21 year-old girl who should have been a Winter Olympic athlete, with her strong, upright stride. This had forced me to walk much faster than I normally would have in such a situation. Also, I had not drunk enough water, relying on the snow on Whitney to fill up my Nalgene bottle, which was a bad idea.

The knowledge of these mistakes had given me some confidence in my Annapurna prep. *If I could stay relaxed in the nights beforehand, and then walk my own walk and stay hydrated, then maybe I could avoid the beleaguered state I had found myself in on Whitney.*

The altitude pills are urine-inducing which had me popping up every hour for another bathroom journey outside. Shankar lay there silently, although I noticed him peering over at me with a quizzical look. The snow was only getting worse. In almost every book I've read on outdoor climbs, expeditions, treks, etc., blind luck has figured prominently in the outcome. That old bitch, *Luck.* Dammit. All I had needed was one more day of clear weather.

I tried deep breathing exercises each time I lay back down. But instead of sleep, adrenaline continued coursing through me. *Maybe I should wait it out today. If there is this much snow at Base Camp, God knows how much there will be up at the Pass. Unlike most trekkers, if my shoes get wet I don't have a spare pair of camp shoes. But if I stay here, I will be utterly miserable; worse yet, struggling to stay warm and dealing with another skull buster headache will probably weaken me.*

Bottom line is I desperately wanted to get out of here. But it could well be dangerous to try the ascent. Of course, I had another option—the one that I had kept in mind the whole way. Turn around and flee the pass—the so-called 'Italian blitzkrieg'. But even that option was fraught. *I don't want to have to cross all those suspension bridges again. Heck, those landslide zones we have been passing through the last couple days would bring pause to the most seasoned mountaineer.*

And what about Shankar? I had worried he would mutiny back at Tal, when he seemed to be indicating he was going forward without me. If I stayed here today, he might just tell me he was going to head on over the Pass. And if I decided to turn around and head back down the Circuit, there was a good chance he would just go the opposite way. *But I cannot let an unruly porter drive such an important decision.*

I've got to stay here. That's my decision. If the weather improves and trekkers can mash the snow down enough, maybe I can get over the Pass tomorrow. As for Shankar, as many lies as have been aimed at me, why can't I try telling one myself?

***

Finally, I began to hear doors shutting and people mingling. People were mobilizing. *This is going to be awkward, but you've got to do it.*

"Shankar," I said, assuming he was awake, "I am sick. I have been vomiting." I made a vomiting motion, pointing out at the bathroom.

"Yes, I know," he said. *Golly damn, am I that good of a liar!* Hopefully not. All my thrashing around in and out of the bed and to the bathroom must have alarmed him.

"I will go down and ask if I can stay tonight."

I headed outside into the night for the fifth time since going to bed. The snow had slackened up to light flurries. When I got to the dining room, it was already packed with familiar faces eating breakfasts that everyone had pre-ordered last night. I sought out the man who seemed to be in charge.

"Sir," I said, pointing to my head. "I am sick. May I stay another night?"

He fumbled through some breakfast tickets, as I wondered if he even understood my question. But then he quickly said, "Yes, probably. But a group has a reservation for that room. You will have to change rooms."

I schlepped back to the room in a heavy frame of mind when I came upon Roger and Elizabeth. I had bonded well with this elderly British couple all the way up. His droll sense of humor and her schoolmarmish ways had added some comity while we all shivered through the evenings in teahouse dining rooms. Fortunately, they had enough courtesy to not ask, "Just where the hell are you going?", as I walked in the opposite direction.

Instead, I asked them, "How big of a problem do you reckon the snow is?" Roger, who was probably the senior member of the Annapurna Circuit at 72 years-old, immediately answered, "I don't believe it's a big issue, at all. Just a bit of a nighttime dusting that should get packed down the minute we all hit the mountain." That was about as unreluctant of an answer as you could ever hope to get out of an Englishman. But it sure as heck made me feel small.

"Good luck," I finally said, and we continued on our separate ways with no further ado.

I gave Shankar the news that we would have to change rooms. Then I lay back down and tried to go back to sleep, which I had about as much chance of doing as I did of ever climbing Everest. My anxious mind was at it again. *When your back is up against the wall, you need to try something. Go one way or another. And I'm not going backwards; that is a last resort. Maybe I could stop at High Base Camp if the snow is a big problem and stay there for the night, although it will be witch-like cold. Or I could come back here and would at least be acclimatized and maybe headache-free?*

"Shankar," I said again, "let's try to make it over the Pass. But we must agree – if I get sick or too much snow, we come back here."

"Yes," he said, and immediately got up. I packed up my considerable supply of clothes and went back down to eat breakfast. It was 4:00 and the dining room was thinned out. Most trekkers had already headed out. I ordered porridge and a scrambled egg, and made it almost halfway through before abandoning each plate.

"Okay, Shankar," I said reaching my hand out to shake hands with him, denoting the importance of the occasion. "We go slow and do our best."

"Yes."

I downed an altitude pill and some Advil, and we headed off. I had arrived at this decision to go for the Pass in a tortured fashion, to be sure. But something told me we were doing the right thing.

CHAPTER 14

Himalayan High

This was really, really cool. First, I was doing something I really do love—walking. From the time I had begun long-distance hiking at age 44, that had always been my ace in the hole. In fact, dating back to my late twenties, I had probably done one activity more than anything else—walking, whether it be in the numerous urban centers I had lived or hiking trails around the world. "*Solvitur ambulando* (Walking solves all)," St. Augustine had memorably written. I couldn't agree more, even if it wasn't completely true.

Friends, girlfriends, roommates, employers, etc. had all been taken aback by my exercise habits over the years. Some thought it showed signs of deprivation, if not outright lunacy. But I'm happy to report that on this score I have proven utterly immune to public opinion. I maintain a deep abiding belief that daily exercise done outdoors—not in a gymnasium—is one of life's great win-win activities.

Despite all my fears, lack of grounding as a wilderness outdoorsman, and problems with cold weather, this conditioning habit had always seen me through the many great footpaths I had chosen to undertake. I had always been able to get up in the morning and make a respectable pace. Now though, I was facing my single most critical walking test ever. The climb would be 3,200 feet, compared to the 4,200 foot climb I had done on Mount Katahdin to complete the Appalachian Trail and another 4,200 foot climb over the Pyrenees to begin El Camino de Santiago. But what lay right in front of me was consistently steeper than those other climbs. Much more significant was the matter of altitude, along with the accompanying oxygen deprivation.

I was wearing an extra-powerful headlamp around my forehead that I had bought especially for the occasion, along with heavy mittens, gators, and an 800 fill down jacket from Eddie Bauer. Snow did indeed cover the breadth of the mountain, as far as I could see. But the snow that remained on the actual rock scree path itself had been reduced to a dusting, just as Roger had suggested it would be.

Ninety-five percent plus of the trekking population was ahead of Shankar and me. But it was encouraging that they weren't all that far ahead. The mountain looked like a torch parade all the way up, dotted as it was with a sea of headlights. *Yes, this really is cool.*

I had read personal narratives of this section that specifically mentioned walking twenty steps, panting with hands on one's knees for a few minutes, and then repeating the exercise. Other accounts mentioned stopping to urinate, only to never be able to get the feeling in their hands again until all the way over the pass. But the minute I got moving, things began to feel natural. Perhaps all the worrying and obsessing I had done the previous couple days had lowered the bar enough to make the drill less difficult. To be sure it was very steep. But soon I felt that assuring sensation of perspiration. After about 300 meters, I sat down on a big boulder and began to remove a couple layers of clothing.

"Bill," Shankar said softly, "I take this (the backpack I was carrying)." Since porters hardly ever change clothing, perhaps Shankar misunderstood my clothing change for weakness.

"No, no," I insisted, and rose again to start climbing.

Lots of short breaks seemed like a viable strategy to make it to the top. The trail ascended precipitously. Despite the fact we were doing switchbacks, gradients in the 40 to 50 degree range popped up in front of us. Soon we were passing trekkers who were propped up against boulders. A competitive attitude surely runs against good outdoor ethics. But it was comforting to know that there were at least a few trekkers who would now be behind me (although I later learned that several of them were no longer technically 'behind', but rather descending back to Base Camp).

"Anybody want a ride?"

However, what we came upon next immediately struck me as practically satanic. "Ride, fifty dollars," I heard coming from somewhere in the dark night. Soon I was able to make out a Nepali man on a horse. "Ride, fifty dollars," he kept repeating. As mentioned before, the Nepali people had impressed me from the beginning as virtually guileless. But this stratagem of trying to coax panting hikers grinding through the very worst part of the Annapurna Circuit to jump on a horse and ride over the Pass seemed like a virtually diabolical temptation. But maybe that's just me. Others might see them like ambulances or fireman— true heroes. In any event, I was to see several such 'horse brokers' barking out "Ride $50", on the way to the pass. And like the hash salesman dotting the streets back in Kathmandu, they weren't all out there without reason. Surely they knew their market.

A little over an hour, three breaks, and 1,400 feet in elevation gain later, the morning sun began peering over the towering Himalayas. Better yet, we soon arrived at *High Base Camp*, a surprisingly impressive structure of sturdy-looking stone buildings. I ran into a big group of Israelis that I had gotten to know. They now all wanted photos, while I stood there like a potted plant, itching to go inside.

"Is it real crowded in there?" I asked them.

"We did not go in," Noa said.

"Let's go have some hot tea," I suggested.

"No, we are going to continue."

"But you are supposed to rest for a while here."

"We want to go."

"Shankar, let's go in."

"No, we continue, Bill."

"Well, okay." *Maybe they're all right about this. My body temperature would probably start falling if I quit moving.*

Thus it was that I continued ascending without anything more than a photograph break, despite having just quickly picked up 1,400 feet in elevation. Guidebooks, websites, experienced trekkers, you name it, universally recommend not ascending more than a thousand feet (300 meters) per day, once you reach 10,000 feet

(3,000 feet). If I really wanted to play it by the book, I would stop here for the night. But now I was a tantalizingly close distance to the top.

The gradients eased up after the High Base Camp; it began to feel more like a normal ascent. The views, however, were anything other than normal. A spectacular mountain panorama of snowy peaks unfolded as the morning sunshine came out. Annapurna III and Gangapurna gleam brilliantly from the west, while Chulu West soars above the other mountains to the east. It didn't take a great romantic to be stirred to the greatest depths by the thought of all the mortals who have gazed in wonderment at these soaring 'cathedrals' through the ages.

***

For the first time since beginning the Circuit, we were not passing along the banks of a powerful, white-capped river roaring through the valley (The reason is that because the Circuit – which habitually tacks between large mountains – now went directly over one). Instead, we walked along a glaciated stream for hundreds of meters. Everyone queued up to cross a frozen wooden bridge. *This must be some of the best water in the world. Why not just fill my empty bottle up, instead of pay God-knows-what price at the next teahouse?* But I was all about doing it by the book in this so very foreign land, so I refrained.

Another mile and 800 feet of elevation gain later, and we arrived at a small wooden hut that served as a teahouse. *I'm coming through!*

The first person I saw was Johannes, a young Swede I had been bantering with the last couple days. "What temperature do you think it is?" I asked.

"Well below freezing," he said. "Make sure you get enough fluids."

The ceiling was not more than 1.80 meters (5'10") in this teahouse. But that was okay. I just wanted some sustenance and ordered garlic soup (recommended at high elevations). I also ordered a bottle of water. When I asked the price, the man blushed a bit before saying – with a semi-apologetic tone – "Four hundred rupees ($5)." *Well, okay. They are learning capitalism. At least they aren't shameless about it.*

I anxiously devoured the bowl of soup. A low-grade migraine had returned. But there was little I could do about it other than drink a lot of water and eventually get down to a lower elevation. Anywhere on this side of the Pass, and I was hopeless in that regard. *It's all about the Pass.*

"You ready?" I asked Shankar.

"Yes."

"How far do you think we are from the top?" I asked Johannes on the way out.

"Maybe 300 meters (1,000 feet) more." That meant we were right now at about 16,800 feet, having ascended approximately 2,200 feet today. Shankar and I started up again when a familiar figure came into view.

"Kate," I yelled forward to the lumbering Australian girl who had become my best friend on the Circuit the last few days. "Good morning."

"Well look who's here," she called back, her freckled face breaking out into a wide smile. Actually, she was being more than chatty. Yesterday, she had figured out from listening to my ruminations about crossing back over the suspension bridges, that I really was considering turning around.

"I've got to ask. Were you the very first person on the mountain this morning?"

"Apart from the guys on the horses," she chortled, which gave both of us a good laugh. It was about 8:00 in the morning; given her 3:30 a.m. start, she would have now been at it four-and-a-half hours. But her strategy – even if it was necessity – had its *bona-fides*. She was picking up altitude at a slower pace than most trekkers. Thus, she was presumably acclimatizing better. Added to that, there was just something I found endearing about a lone woman out here struggling so valiantly at something she also wasn't very good at. But she certainly seemed to be carrying it all off with better cheer than I had managed.

"Well hang in there," I said, as Shankar and I did a loop around her. I would probably have enjoyed her company for the rest of the way up. But I had learned very early on the Appalachian Trail that long-distance hikers were habitually more loyal to the task ahead, than any particular trekker. At first it had struck me as selfish when hikers, whose company I was enjoying, had left me behind. But when I started doing it myself, it just seemed like the natural order of things.

"Save me some champagne at the bottom," Kate called out.

"Sure thing."

***

In one sense, altitude mountain sickness is no mystery—it's a direct function of altitude. However, by most accounts it is an entirely rogue actor in just who it strikes. AMS essentially causes fluid to accumulate in tissues of the lungs or around the brain as the body is deprived of adequate oxygen. Even Sherpas, for all their legendary lung capacity, have been fatal victims on countless occasions.

"The fact is that most people probably get some type of mild altitude sickness up there," one veteran British trekker had told me. "Effectively what you're doing is making a break for it up there." *Making a break for it.* To be quite honest, that was looking more and more like a better analogy. Because what we were doing— ascending 3,200 feet from an already high elevation of 14,600 feet, with little in the way of acclimatization—was a one day strut into a netherworld.

Up until our hut break, I had been running on adrenaline. Indeed, that same adrenaline had seen me through many a tough day on other long-distance hikes. But it was getting ready to run into something the likes of which I had never before encountered. I slowly began taking less confident steps, without even realizing it. My buoyant mood at the pace I had been making began to unconsciously unravel. All through the ascent I had been working on controlling my breathing, hoping to inhale as much as possible through my nose, instead of mouth, in order to conserve on adrenaline. But now I fell into deep, labored breaths. My full stride morphed into a half steps; soon I was deliberately placing one foot at the end of the other.

Let's face it. We were up here. The weak glimpse of sunshine we had gotten just an hour earlier had been replaced by leaden gray skies and snow flurries. It had never gotten close to freezing this morning, and now I was feeling it.

"Shankar," I yelled forward, "I need clothes."

Shankar this morning had the gait of a fugitive who really was making a break for it. At the sound of my summons, he reluctantly set down the backpack. I reached in and grabbed my heavy Icelandic sweater, which meant I would now be ascending in six layers. But I still couldn't get warm, so I threw down some more Advil. *It's too cold to take a break. I've got to get out of here.*

So we continued, now moving slower than ever. I had heard there were several false summits before hitting Thorung La Pass; perhaps that was even a good thing to keep psychologically urging us forward. Up ahead to the left, was a peak that I kept leering at; I felt pretty sure it was Thorung Peak. *If that's the peak, the pass has to be nearby. I can make it there.* But now I was palpably getting weaker. And weak and slow are one thing; dizziness is another. That's how I was beginning to feel in this unholy union of altitude and cold.

***

"Shankar," I called forward and hit both knees in the snow. There was no way to urinate on this barren mountain other than out in the wide open. Given that the altitude pills were urine-inducing, I had already stopped several times on the way up. Now I just propped up on one knee and relieved myself. *This is the ballgame. It's all about the next half-hour.* With that thought, I grabbed the medicine bottle and threw down another Diamox. *To hell with the side effects.*

But to go much further, it was essential that I somehow relax. It now appeared I had made a major strategic mistake this morning. I should have taken long breaks at both High Base Camp and the last teahouse, instead of just the one hurried break. That would have left me in better condition to 'make a break for it' up here. Now at approximately 17,300 feet, having tried Ibuprofen, altitude pills, extra clothes, and now an unrelaxing break, I had only one ace-in-the-hole left to play—take Shankar up on his oft-repeated offer. "Shankar, can you carry my backpack to the top?" I humbly asked.

As mentioned earlier, as best I could tell, Shankar ignored

my request. And not because he was insulted by it, either. From the beginning of our time together, he had offered to carry the smaller backpack that I was toting, in addition to the larger one. My repeated rejections of his prior offers were proof enough that this wasn't just a gratuitous request. There was only one reason I could think of for his surprising non-acceptance. *He's hurting too.* However, most Nepali porters would rather perish than show weakness. His silence was merely the 'dog that didn't bark'.

Now, through a process of elimination, the only course of action I could think of was to keep on ascending. We started up again. At this point it was all about willpower overriding instinct. But after arriving at the top of the next hill, I looked up and all that came into view was yet more snowy hills on three sides. It really wasn't even clear which direction the trail led, because all the trekkers ahead of us had zoomed out of sight. But now the idea of lying down for another break seemed futile. I would only get colder, and it had not helped me catch my breath. No, I absolutely had to find the strength to see me through the next half-hour. The question I had been debating internally was this: *If I pass out here in this snow, will my breathing normalize? Or not?*

I stood doubled over my two trekking poles, in the middle of the Annapurna Circuit, breathing deeply. Perhaps I could be accused of engaging in the well-known hiker's art of '*Yogi-ing*' (getting somebody to do something without actually asking for it). To be sure, I was not being theatrical. But I did halfway expect to hear Shankar's soft voice saying, "Bill, give me backpack." I had been in this contorted position for several minutes, when I heard a different voice.

"Bill, that's not going to get you to the top." It was Kate, in what can only be described as another chapter of the tortoise and the hare.

CHAPTER 15

NOT ROB SLATER

"I summit, or I die. Either way I win." Those were the immortal words of my erstwhile close friend, the late Rob Slater (1960-1995).

Rob had been one of the first friends I had made after moving to Chicago in 1985 to enter the commodities business. We met on the city bus, which we both took downtown every morning to the Chicago Board of Trade.

Obviously those words of his above don't stand out for their humility. However, Rob did show some innate modesty. It wasn't for a full year after we met that another person on the trading floor sidled up to me and asked, "Are you a climber also?"

"What are you talking about?" I had asked him.

"Well that guy you're always talking to is a world-class mountain climber."

"You're kidding," I said. "Rob Slater?"

"Yeah."

When I asked Rob about it on the bus the next morning, he sheepishly spilled out the truth. Later he showed me a front-page article in the Wall Street Journal, touting this mountain climbing protégé who had entered the commodities business in Chicago.

"Does This Man Crave Risk?" the blaring headline had asked. Good question and perhaps the words above indicate such an inclination.

However, I wouldn't actually call Rob recklessly risk-prone. What he did evince was the capacity to blot out all else in favor of a few deeply held pursuits. In fact, anybody who was around him was very cognizant of his three great passions: becoming a successful trader, Cindy Hickey, and the summit of K-2 in Pakistan. To be sure, all three were lofty goals.

"I want to make it so bad," he kept confiding to me about his trading. "If I can make it as a trader, I can go places no human has ever been." Alas, like so many aspiring traders, he ultimately failed. To be quite honest, he just wasn't a big enough asshole for the cutthroat culture of a trading floor.

Cindy Hickey was a more unusual case. She also traded at the Chicago Board of Trade during Rob's tenure there. And she certainly didn't lack for attractiveness. However, the way Rob went on incessantly about her to absolutely anybody who would listen, you would have thought she was *Helen of Troy*. On the other hand, it wasn't clear she really even knew who he was. Finally, one sympathizer humanely decided to intervene and arranged for Rob to take Cindy out to dinner. In retrospect, the results were probably predictable. Their date fell flat. "She just thought he was a total weirdo," the intermediary later told me (as a consolation prize, he named his cat, 'Cindy'). If you ask me though, it was her loss, as he was one of the most authentic guys I ever have had the privilege to meet.

But now that Rob's trading dreams were gone and Cindy Hickey was off the radar screen, it was that third dream that became his lifetime obsession. *K-2.* I would see him after work in our Lincoln Park neighborhood in Chicago in the middle of high-intensity workouts. Rob would gush rhapsodically about the drama and horrors of K-2 in far-off Pakistan. At the time, I had never even heard of it, although I'm now aware of just how legendary this Himalayan monster is in mountaineering circles. "That summit, that's where it's at for me," he gushed. "There's no other place." He quit his job in Chicago and returned back to his native state of Colorado to train fulltime for the quest. It was at the airport in Denver when leaving for his lifetime's mission, that a reporter recorded his memorable quote.

Rob's expedition team of eight included the renowned Scottish climber, Allison Hargreaves. Just months before, she had generated a national controversy in the British press with her bid to become the first female to do an unsupported summit of Mount Everest. The debate had centered on whether Hargreaves, who had two children aged three and five, was being selfish to take on such an inherently risky climb. Nonetheless, in May, 1995, she pulled it off, returning to Great Britain with great fanfare. "One of the greatest climbs of all time," gushed the *London Times*. But those who knew her weren't surprised at her success. After all, this same woman had done the toughest climb in Europe, *Eiger North* in the Alps, while heavily pregnant with her first child.

That very same summer, Hargreaves was also part of a group that received a coveted permit to do K-2 on the China-Pakistan border. Rob Slater, four Europeans, and two New Zealanders rounded out her expedition team. More incendiary debate ensued in the British press, but Hargreaves was again undaunted.

By late that summer, the expedition team readied to climb up the final shelf of K-2. However, one of the New Zealanders, Peter Hillary, son of the renowned Edmund Hillary, began to have doubts. He noticed an ominous bank of clouds building up in the direction of the Chinese border. What's more, he felt something less tangible – a feeling of unease and disquiet. "Come on up, come on up," Allison Hargreaves kept yelling down at him. But the words that reverberated through his mind as he stood there before this ice wall were those of his famous father – "Don't be afraid to stand alone." Hillary turned around.

However, Hargreaves, Slater, and the other four members of their expedition team (one had already turned around before Hillary, but still died on the way down) continued up. In *Into Thin Air*, Jon Krakauer makes the case that true mountain climbers really don't respect another climber until they've gotten into a situation in which all safety valves are closed off and everything is on the line. At approximately 6:45 p.m. on August 13, 1995 the expedition party of six reached the summit. They radioed down to jubilantly report their success. Unfortunately, torrid Manchurian winds began to brew, threatening their position on the summit. The descent off K-2 is infamous in the climbing community; fully 25% of the climbers who make the summit die on the way down. On this day, the high winds ultimately reached 100 miles per hour. All six climbers lost their purchase on the mountain, falling to their deaths (Hillary successfully fought for his life in the storm down at Base Camp II).

I was living in London at the time and vividly remember how the tragedy dominated the news on *BBC* (British Broadcasting Corporation) for almost a week. The coverage again centered on the Hargreaves family, with their now motherless three and five year-old sons. "How could I have stopped her?" her husband, James Ballard, asked rhetorically. "I loved Allison because she wanted to climb the highest peak her skills would allow her to. That's who she was. I don't regret her going to K-2. All I can be sure of is that she was as happy as she could have been at the moment she died."

***

Now as I stood slumped almost helplessly over my trekking poles within a half-hour or so of Thorung La Pass, the thought of my old buddy, Rob Slater, again came into my mind. While socially compatible, we had very difficult philosophies about clearing high elevations. I was a typical Annapurna trekker. I had wanted to see the Himalayas, and the Annapurna Circuit had seemed like the most interactive, authentic way. And now I badly wanted to make it over Thorung La Pass. But I was not willing to do anything that willingly put my life on the line.

Besides being cold, I was now beginning to feel sleepy to the point of slightly drunk. I simply lacked any real-life experience to know whether I was in a true predicament. I did, however, remember a couple salient points from Krakauer's book. First, at a seriously high elevation such as Everest or K-2, a climber – even an acclimatized climber – has the mental capacity of a child. In fact, if a helicopter dropped an expert mountain climber off at the summit of Everest, he (she) would be dead within minutes. Now once again, what I was doing wasn't remotely a challenge of that caliber. But some mental impairment probably was taking place, even at these elevations. However, Krakauer's book also vividly pointed up the horrific condition that some of the climbers on Everest found themselves in, yet who nonetheless managed to make it through. So that horribly banal cliché—we are stronger than we know—apparently is really true.

The mass of trekkers which had been bunched up so closely the last few days appeared to have developed a gigantic fault line in the middle. The stronger trekkers were nowhere in sight after having galloped ahead, while the weaker brothers and sisters were now well back. I, myself, was in reality just such a weaker brother. But my brethren were hiking the smarter hike by pacing themselves on this great climb, while I had maxed out from the opening step this morning, a la *Icarus* (who maxed out in his waxed wings and plunged into the Aegean sea).

I slowly straightened myself up and began walking. Knowing that the guidebook had been generally reliable as to elevations, despite all the false summits, the pass had to be getting close. It just had to. Any pretense of either strength or style was now long gone. The only thing I could do was take baby steps expending the minimal amount of energy. Belatedly I was playing it smart.

In *High Exposure* Magazine, David Brashears points out that at 17,600 feet the oxygen-deficient atmosphere is not life-sustaining. Your body literally consumes itself for energy, a kind of slow biological death. You are very much 'on the clock' at this point. But once I got to this elevation, rather than having 8,000, 10,000, or more feet to ascend like the Rob Slaters and Allison Hargreaves and Jon Krakauers of this world, I needed a mere 168 feet in elevation gain to clear the Pass at 17,768 feet.

Finally, I turned a dogleg in the trail and saw a big post ('stupa') in the ground with pennants hanging off of it. Trekkers were crowded around it gleefully taking photographs. That's about all I can tell you about it, though. I had every intention to be faithful to the vow I had made on the way up that I would not even slow down at the top, but rather

Getting as high as possible!

continue on in order to get down to a more habitable elevation.

Amazingly, there is a small wooden hut at Thorung La Pass. But I had no interest in it either. However, Shankar started doing a beeline towards the hut. "Shankar," I called forward, "let's go. We eat at bottom." But he didn't break his stride until arriving at the wooden hut, where he dropped the backpack and walked straight in. I followed suit.

The hut was crowded and chaotic, with a roof well shy of 6-feet tall. However, the mood was festive. I predictably ordered a garlic soup and found a seat at a crowded table, anxious that I wasn't completely out of the woods yet. Two gay women from California prompted me to chat, which proved to be helpful. And you know us damn males – give us a chance and we sure will tell you about our sojourns.

"I had an even worse migraine on Mount Whitney (in California)," I told them, "but was much more out of breath here."

"What else are you going to remember besides your headache?" one of the ladies asked.

"The false summits."

"That first light this morning was ethereal," the other lady said.

The soup came. Technically, there probably was some garlic in there, although it tasted predominantly like snow melt. But I poured it down and was probably able to gain some sustenance. "Let's go, Shankar," I said urgently the minute I had drained the bowl.

This time I was good to my word, completely eschewing the still-crowded celebration post. I had heard the descent was even steeper than the ascent. Indeed, this was initially the case. But immediately I felt like I was on more solid footing, and bolted down the mountain. *This is going to be fun.*

The treading in the snow was slick, but not dangerous. The sun, eerily invisible on the far side of the mountain, dominated this side. A fresh migraine broke out in my head. But at this point, it felt almost felt like a badge of honor.

"Hey Kate," I chortled, when we again came upon my Australian comrade who had continued right on over the top, "why didn't you wait at the top for a photo with me?"

"There was hardly room," she laughed. Her freckled face seemed to have turned watermelon red in the glowing late morning sunshine. She was visibly struggling with the downhill. But again she seemed unruffled about it.

"Let's do the cakewalk to Jomsom together tomorrow," I suggested to Kate.

"Sure thing," she called forward.

Alas, this was to be the last time I ever saw Kate. For when I asked around about her that evening, I ran into a German man who related a moving tale. Kate had struggled valiantly all afternoon and finally brought the ship to port in Muktinath just before dark. No danger, but it had been a 14 hour day without taking a single flat step. She had hurried to a pay phone to make the ritual celebratory phone call to her boyfriend in Australia. However, her boyfriend's best friend answered the phone and proceeded to ruin the rest of her trip, if not her life. Her boyfriend had been found passed out in his house and was under full life-support. Despite the fact that this was her first trip out of her home country and she was already booked for a month's long package in India after this, Kate immediately arranged a private taxi to Jomsom, a flight from there to Kathmandu, and then home to Australia.

On so many travels, it is ultimately the people one meets that make or break the trip. Of course the geography in Nepal is so magisterial that it is obviously about more than that. But the type of people who travel from parts yonder to embrace such a daunting land are not easily forgotten.

***

Shankar now seemed surprised at his client. The reluctant, almost moping, figure of the last week-and-a-half suddenly morphed into one of the fastest and most energetic trekkers on the mountain. It had been so long since I had gone downhill that it was all a novelty; I zoomed past scores of trekkers in the snow-covered downhill.

What a difference just a few minutes makes!

The hard rays of the late morning sun bore down on my skull, only increasing the intensity of my migraine. I stopped to pour down water every ten minutes or so. But this migraine was of such glory that it was not to be denied. Nonetheless, my mood was a wonderful mélange of relief and exhilaration, and I continued at full speed. It almost seemed like an afternoon on the ski slopes. The path was not always clearly delineated, and we couldn't help but sprint down some of the zig-zags. Trekkers were pirouetting and falling all over the place. But the snow was like mashed potatoes and it was mostly to laugh about. After all, everybody could breathe deeply again.

However, not everybody found such levity in it. I came upon a couple from Hong Kong that I had gotten to know in my sick downtime back in Jagat. The woman, who was a slave to trekking fashion with all her silk scarves, leather boots, and fur coat, was frozen in seeming horror over a 'precipice' in the trail. It was really just a snowy steep patch of about 10 feet, but she looked like she was getting ready to take the first step on a tightrope between two skyscrapers in New York. "Head first," I playfully called back up to her; but my sense of humor was vastly underappreciated.

And perhaps I should have piped down because of all the problems I had had on the long ascent. But even Roger and Elizabeth, the older British couple, seemed out of sorts about the whole thing. "Come on – straight down for *the Queen*," I called out to them while passing. But the formerly imperturbable Englishman said, "I do not like this," with great emphasis. I finally just 'zipped it' (my mouth) and settled in to enjoy the descent and my migraine.

A 5,300 foot descent is significant by any measure, when you consider that the tallest mountain in the world is 29,002 feet. Yes, your lungs get a break; it's your knees that move squarely into the crossfire. But lactic acid beats mountain sickness any day and I reveled in checking out the new scenery. The snowy Dhaulagiri range, which Maurice Herzog's party had originally planned to ascend before switching to Annapurna, beckons in the distance. The surprising thing, though, was how very different the landscape was on this side of Thorung La Pass. Instead of steep, snow-capped peaks, we now looked out on expansive vistas of brown, arid hills leading down to wide open valleys. However, perhaps I shouldn't have been surprised, given the intense sunlight dominating the horizon.

After almost 4,000 feet of descent, we came to the first human outpost at *Chabarbu*, which had a couple wooden shacks serving food. The nausea from my migraine was overwhelmed by hunger (I had eaten very little for the last few days, despite the fact you need more calories at high elevations). I quickly devoured a plate of chicken fried rice. We then continued the remaining 1,400 feet down, which now seemed almost like a drop in the bucket.

On the final part of the descent, Shankar and I caught up with the big French group. Their tense march yesterday along the narrow banks of the Marsyangdi in the morning, and gritty determination to reach High Base Camp yesterday afternoon, had been replaced by jovial chanting. I put them in stitches with my rendition of *FrereJacques*, the nursery rhyme about the sleepy French boy, long since famous the world over. They sallied back with their own *Forest Gump* imitations.

Our destination was *Muktinath*, which up until now had simply been a place I had to get to on the toughest day on the Annapurna Circuit. But actually Muktinath is well known in its own regard as one of Nepal's holiest places. A sacred complex of pagodas and temples that attracts Hindus and Buddhists from all over Asia lies right at the foot of the steep descent.

Just as we entered the outskirts of the town, the big French group hung a sharp left.

"Where are you going?" Veronique asked.

"To try to find a room," I answered.

"But you must see this temple," she exhorted.

"Well, I guess we should follow the French on something cultural."

"Yes, remember that."

We tiptoed behind them into the temple, which featured the hush common to cathedral visits in Europe. Interestingly, in Nepal or India a person is categorized more by whether or not they are a person of strong faith, than by the particular religion. In the United States, however, we would be more likely to label a person as Catholic, for example, whether they were devout or lapsed.

We did not tarry in the temple anywhere near as long as the French group. Muktinath, itself, was actually a real town, as opposed to just a collection of teahouses. As I wandered happily around town, I ran into dozens of the glorious cast of trekkers from around the world who populate this great Circuit, *Annapurna*. The extra spring in their step was palpable – a kind of 'we've done it', as they loped all over the village.

I was greatly looking forward to the further long descents which lay ahead. However, we would quickly see that others did not have the same philosophy. Also, I was getting ready to learn quite a bit more about the 'gentleman' who had been carrying my backpack the last ten days.

CHAPTER 16

Turmoil

"Bill, jeep to Jomsom," Shankar said. "We take?"

"Why take a jeep?" I asked with indignation. He didn't respond. Rather he just looked away as if peeved. But then he said, "I take jeep in Jomsom." *He's going to take the jeep when we get to Jomsom. Isn't that quitting?*

"I'm supposed to do *Everest Base Camp*," he suddenly explained. Strange that I hadn't heard anything about that before, as much as we had all talked about the trek up to Everest Base Camp (Also a popular trek. However, you can't see the actual summit of Mount Everest. You have to go to a nearby mountain.)

It was the morning after the big day, and I was wandering around looking for a water station to get discounted water, and to see where everybody was. I ran into Johannes again.

"A jeep is coming by to pick us up at 9:00 this morning," Johannes informed me. "Do you want to ride along to Jomsom?"

"Why are you riding?" I asked. "It should be a cakewalk."

"Gabby (his Mexican wife) had a very difficult day yesterday," he said in a low, confiding voice. "It was a bit much."

"Hey," I said in a buoyant tone. "Those are the best stories— somebody who cuts it close."

Mighty glaciers meet their match in these arid regions

"Yeah, well" he acknowledged, without agreeing, "we're going back to Kathmandu. She's still shaken up by it."

Shankar and I headed out of town alone. This was a completely different atmosphere from yesterday when we had departed with reams of puckered-up hikers into the pitch black early morning cold. We now followed the dirt road which ran across a dusty tableland, overseeing the cavernous valley. This side of the mountain had the wide open look of the American West – a certain stark, saline quality – that I found fetching. However, the scenery we were gazing out on was more than just another aesthetically pleasing landscape. Rather, it was the lower edge of what – in terms of actual life and death – may well be the most important geological region in the world – *the Tibetan Plateau.*

Tibetan Plateau – Future of the World?

If the 20th century was the century of petro-conflict, the 21st century may end up being that of *aqua-conflict*. Why? For two reasons. First, water is infinitely more valuable than oil in an ultimate sense. And secondly, there are alarming indications that the world's water supply has begun to significantly diminish. And some of the strongest evidence may lie right here in the highest and largest plateau in the world, the Tibetan Plateau.

The glaciers from this plateau give birth to Asia's largest and most legendary rivers, from the Yangtze and Yellow Rivers, to the Mekong and Ganges. Over the course of history, these rivers have nurtured entire civilizations, even inspiring religions. All told, some *two billion people* in a dozen countries – nearly one-third of the world's population – depend on rivers fed by the snow and ice of this plateau region.

Just consider the case of the Yangtze. Its source lies in the Tibetan plateau. Yet it flows 6,300 kilometers (4,200 miles) all the way to the East China Sea where it enters the harbor at the Chinese megapolis, Shanghai. The Yangtze accounts for 40% of China's freshwater resources, 70% of its rice production, 50% of grain production, 70% of fishery production, and 40% of its GDP. Yet the glacier that feeds the Yangtze is in clear retreat.

On the southern side of the Tibetan plateau, cities like New Delhi, which lies 300 kilometers (180 miles) south of the Himalayan glaciers are now experiencing water demand in excess of supply by over 300 million gallons a day. In large swaths of Delhi, its denizens spend their days in mad pursuit of water trucks carrying their lifeline.

"For all their seeming might and immutability," says Lonnie Thompson, a glaciologist at Ohio State University, "the irony is that the Himalayan glaciers are more exposed to climate change than almost anywhere in the world." These glaciers, which lie on the so-called "roof of the world", melt twice as fast as the surface. Despite the fact that the Tibetan Plateau has an *average* elevation of 15,000 feet, one-sixth of it is now covered by desert. Temperatures in these high elevations are rising twice as fast as in surface regions.

If the current trends hold, Chinese scientists now believe that 40% of the Tibetan Plateau's glaciers could disappear by 2050. And after that? "Full glacier disappearance is inevitable," says Yao Tandong, a glaciologist at China's Institute of Tibetan Plateau Research. In other words, China's greatest rivers would be depleted under this scenario. Given that China has less water than Canada, but forty times as many people, the potential ecological catastrophe defies the mind. Effectively humans would be forced to make do off whatever falls out of the sky.

Unsurprisingly, China, the premier practicioner of power politics for the last 5,000 years, has an ace in the hole. The sources of most of these major rivers lie within its borders. The government has drawn up detailed plans to divert the water that now flows from those rivers into other countries, keeping it in China instead. In fact, one source lies right where the China-India conflict broke out in 1962. Pakistan and India also share water sources, which could explosively increase tensions between the two nuclear-powered antagonists.

So is this all shaping up to be a geological version of *Apocalypse Now?* To be sure, given my lack of scientific background I'm a pretty 'easy lay' when I read these stories. But the majority of scientists from around the globe feel like critical mass is now approaching. Heck, just feeling the intensity of the sun since we had made it over to this side of the mountains was enough to convince me of the enormous havoc that temperature change could wreak in this plateau region lying straight ahead.

***

Periodically, we would hear blaring horns followed by small local buses, crammed with trekkers and backpacks attached to the roof.

"That looks awful," I observed, but again got no reaction from Shankar. However, I was able to enjoy the walk plenty enough in silence. My grim persona of just a day or two back now seemed light years ago.

We were pleasantly descending over 3,000 feet today. After an hour of leisurely strolling, we came to a fork in the road. The road to the right appeared to lead down to a community that had the fetching appearance of an American Southwest adobe-style pueblo. I began to head in that direction. But Shankar corrected me and pointed left. "Bill, this road." I followed his cue, only to belatedly find out from the Scottish girls that I had bypassed the coolest town in the valley. *Kagbeni* had been the hub of the salt trade across the Tibetan border for centuries. However, the really painful part though was that Kagbeni had a McDonalds, although it was tastefully named, *YacDonalds,* because of the yak meat served in there.

Instead of a traipse through those delights, what we got on our route was an old-fashioned dust storm. I later learned that the long river bed we entered in the approach to Jomsom is renowned for pulverizing any and all passers-thru in the afternoon. For that reason, trekkers habitually stay in Kagbeni and approach the river valley into Jomsom in the early morning hours. The gale force winds were of such brute force that not only was the lanky Georgia boy rocking all over the place, but his Nepali porter was pitching about as well. Which made me wonder something that had been occurring with greater frequency—*how many times has Shankar really done the Annapurna Circuit?*

My light mood of the morning quickly dissipated as I got bullied all over the wide open field. Shankar and I made no effort to communicate or even walk together, as I tried hovering closer towards the banks of the gorge. *He would not steal my backpack. I really don't think so.*

***

Jomsom is the largest village on the Annapurna Circuit. Therein lay its importance. For starters, it had an airport that allowed trekkers easy access to and from these mountains. It was also rumored to have a functioning cash machine, which I desperately needed. The higher prices near the top had virtually depleted my available cash supply. Veteran trekkers and guides had given me definitive assurances that there would be a machine here in Jomsom. "As long as the wind doesn't knock out the electricity," they had all hedged themselves. Indeed, there were no flights out of the airport after 10:30 in the morning due to the heavy winds.

Shankar and I followed the river to where the town divided. "Which way?" I asked. He hesitated before walking straight. But then after 50 meters or so, he turned around and we retraced our steps. I followed him across the bridge. Soon we found ourselves walking down a main street worthy of the infamous Dodge City in the 19th century Wild, Wild, American West.

"Which hotel do you recommend?"

"I take bus to Pokhara," Shankar said.

He was referring to the resort city of Pokhara, which lies fetchingly at the foot of the Himalayas. All trekkers on the Annapurna Circuit eventually end up there, and I was looking forward to it myself. But it was a two day bus ride, which I didn't want any part of. I had come to Nepal to walk.

My contract with Shankar was for 16 days, and this was day 13. He was skimping out and there wasn't a thing in the world I could do about it. *Getting ripped off is just what happens to Westerners— especially Americans.* Of course, that kind of laid-back attitude probably doesn't do future foreign trekkers any good, because it makes them easier victims also.

As for what was going on with Shankar, it didn't take an especially subtle mind to divine his purposes. He was trying to 'game' me. Many trekkers had long porter contracts for side trips after completing the Circuit. But I had no interest in taking any more side trips with this, or any other, porter. My goal was to complete the Annapurna Circuit. We had at least four more days on the Circuit, including huge descents and then more ascents through notable terrain.

If Shankar leaves, then I've gotten a bad deal. But I can handle what lies ahead. And I damn sure ain't going to tip him for welching out on me.

"Are you taking the night bus?" I asked Shankar.

"Do not know," he said. And when I began crisscrossing the main street checking out beds in the various teahouses, Shankar stayed right on my heels. He jumped into the conversation at one and arranged a place for both myself and himself to stay. *So he's bluffing.*

I now wandered up to the cash machine. This was a big moment. Plenty of times while abroad, and never more than here, I have wondered what in the world I would do if the machine either ate my card or denied me cash. I was relieved to hear the clicking sound, as it worked like a Swiss watch. In fact, I went back again that night for more because there was said to be no other place in the mountains that a foreigner could get cash. This gave me the flexibility I needed to begin considering other notable treks in the area, once I got finished with the Annapurna Circuit.

***

"Bill, can we talk?"

"Sure," I said to the German girl, Greta's guide. Of course, guides generally had much better English than porters to begin with. And this particular guide was especially personable and had proven to be quite knowledgeable about all aspects of the Annapurna Circuit. Shankar frequently seemed to be tracking him, probably looking for clues, as well as cues.

"Why do you not take Shankar to Pokhara?" he asked me. I guess you could say it was touching that he would try to look out for another porter.

"Because I am walking all the way and might do another trek after the Circuit," I explained. "His contract will end before that."

"Shankar want to trek."

"We have three days left on the contract. He can do what he wants."

The Nepalis may be the most likable people I have ever met. But thank God, they aren't as cagey as the Indians or Chinese. This whole gig was becoming more clear to me. It was about money, pure and simple. Shankar wanted me to extend his contract beyond the 16 day limit. But I was looking very much forward to the freedom of being on my own again, just as I had been on all my previous hikes. And I was planning to take another route into the mountains upon completion of the Annapurna Circuit. The last thing I was going to do was extend his contract; in fact I was perfectly willing to let him bolt right now and renege on the balance of the contract. And that, I presumed, improved my bargaining position.

But soon I began to realize that getting rid of him was not going to be as simple as I had thought.

"Shankar," I asked him, "what time does the night bus leave?" My question was a bit mischievous because I knew he was not going to take the night bus. He shrugged his shoulder and said, "Bus in morning."

A further problematic issue came up. Greta's guide again approached me out on the dirt road where I was checking out all the cowboy town's western-style facades. "Bill," he asked me, "do you know there is a checkpoint outside town?"

A checkpoint. Okay. That in itself wasn't a big deal. I had not seen any police-state tendencies here in Nepal. But to get through the checkpoint I would need to show the two trekking permits. Up until now, Shankar had been handling these permits. However, now that I thought about it, he had kept them in the smaller backpack that I had been carrying. I hurried back to the teahouse, while Shankar stayed huddled up on the other side of the street leering at me.

Perhaps it was even a 'cat who ate the canary' stare he was giving me; for when I opened up the pocket of the backpack where the permits had been all along, they were no longer there. The plot had now thickened.

BILL WALKER

CHAPTER 17

Cutting the Chord

I sat with a group of Americans at breakfast marveling over airplanes threading the needle through the surrounding mountains on their takeoff and landing from the airport runway, which lay right beside the hotel. Shankar was conspicuously absent from the dining room, no longer obsequiously taking my orders and bringing food. I had never cottoned on it the role of 'master' to begin with; it was a relief to be done with it.

After breakfast, I walked outside where buses were being loaded up 'Nepali-style', for long journeys to Pokhara. Shankar stood nearby.

I walked over and said, "Shankar, The guidebook recommends leaving early to beat the heavy winds. I am going." He did not respond and we again drifted apart. But then he came back over and said, "Bill, much traffic on this road. You should not walk." But I was no longer the exhausted traveler who proved to be such as easy victim for his boss, Vijay.

"I'm walking," I said plainly. "We need to exchange backpacks and I need the trekking permits." He said nothing so I went inside the porter's room and grabbed my backpack. I had decided Shankar and I fell into the never-should-have-married and immediately-need-to-get-a-divorce category. But when I got back outside, Shankar said, "Bill, I walk to *Tukuche* and take bus there."

"Let's go then," I said. What else could I say? Sure, Nepali porters may be the toughest people in the world. But once you had hired one, they were also a dependent child of yours.

So it was, we left Jomsom together – two unhappy campers. I had really hoped to cut the umbilical cord right here and had been looking forward to a 'freedom march' on the way out of town. *The trekking papers?* To think I was in the world's greatest mountain range, replete with spectacular scenery and adventurous trekkers from all over the world, and was now obsessed with some damn trekking papers.

However, perhaps I shouldn't have been surprised at such friction developing with a Sherpa. In *Annapurna: A Woman's Place*, Arlene Blum repeatedly referred to the utter turmoil that rebellious Sherpas had wreaked on their expedition. Five porters had deserted early on. And when they got to High Camp III, all tensions flared out into the open.

"This is the worst expedition I've ever been on," one Sherpa had shouted at her.

"What's the matter?" Blum had asked.

"Equipment is very bad. Food is very bad. Members are very bad."

The head Sherpa tried to intervene; but then he, too, became indignant. "Members must carry loads or we must hire more Sherpas."

"Outrageous," she responded. "We're carrying as much as the Sherpas, even though they are stronger."

A heated debate had then ensued over who the eventual owner would be of the high-insulation sleeping bags purchased for the expedition. When the Sherpas were told they could not have them, they stormed out of High Camp, shouting furiously over their shoulders, "See you in Kathmandu." Blum was then forced to spend two days chasing them all the way back down at Base Camp.

In her memoir, she chose to wax philosophically about all the turbulence. "Complaints about food and equipment are not unusual on expeditions and frequently mean that the Sherpas want more money."

***

We came to a fork in the trail with a suspension bridge veering off to the left. Shankar bolted over the bridge, while I hesitated as usual. But in this case, there was an additional reason for my reluctance – my map did not list a bridge crossing here.

"Shankar, is this correct?" I called out. Again, he looked around with a stern look, before slowly retreating back over the bridge. We continued on down the road, where we soon saw other trekkers. I was beginning to think that Shankar needed to walk the whole way for the same exact reason as me—so he could say he has in fact done the entire Annapurna Circuit at least once!

We were now back down below 10,000 feet, and my glum mood didn't budge as we bore into the increasingly intense morning sun. When I stopped to urinate and drink water, Shankar launched his offensive. No, he didn't unload a fusillade of blows at my long, thin physique (although he probably could have).

"Bill, you are supposed to pay my bus to Pokhara," he said angrily. "and it is *law* you give porter tips." Both ends of that compound sentence happened to be flat-out lies. Vijay had actually made it perfectly clear that my porter fee of $407 included the bus fare for both Shankar and myself to Pokhara upon completion of the Circuit (In other words, Shankar was actually supposed to pay for *my* bus ticket to Pokhara when we got through). And I would have surely heard if there really was a law requiring the tipping of porters. Nonetheless, my overwhelming instinct in a situation like this is to defuse tensions, rather than ratchet them up. This seemed especially crucial in a country with a completely different culture such as Nepal's.

"I'm going to give you a tip, Shankar," I caved. "But remember, Vijay gave you the money for both of us to take the bus to Pokhara. So you do not need any money for that."

"The bus to Pokhara costs 1,800 to 2,400 rupees ($25 to $30)," he said.

"It does not cost anywhere near that much," I countered.

Things continued spiraling downhill as Shankar pressed, "Bill, how much you pay Vijay?" I briefly thought about telling him. But then I decided the question was nothing but trouble and let it go. Vijay had told me most of my porter fee would actually go to the porter; however, Shankar's suspicious probe began to make me wonder. So once again, the whole arrangement just looked like it was misbegotten from the get-go. I was simply going to have to pay my way out of the mess. I decided I would give him a $50 (4,000 rupee) tip-ransom.

In a little over an hour we were in Marpha, renowned as the 'Apple Capital of Nepal'. But my appetite for sightseeing had soured and we continued on, although we now at least had the consolation of pulling apples off trees and sinking our teeth in. Two more hours later we got to *Tukuche*, where this mini-drama was to come to a close.

Greta and her well-spoken guide were there eating lunch and we joined them. Greta was a physical therapist back in Germany, and quite obviously had arranged her trip with Teutonic discipline.

Last night she had told me that her guidebook recommended tipping porters $3 per day. We moved inside to get out of the hot sun. Greta's guide again came up and said, "Bill, Shankar take bus here." Something told me that this time it was the truth. *But the permits?*

Greta and her guide finished lunch and headed off. Now it was just Shankar and me around the dining table

"Shankar, are you leaving?" I asked.

"Yes," he softly said, looking slightly embarrassed. The situation was, after all, a bit perverted. But then he added another fig leaf, that by now was easy to recognize as a ploy. "Bill, next town, Kalopani, too far today."

"But the map says only a few more hours from here," I said. "I like walking late."

Is this the first Nepali porter in history that is lazy?" Most likely the answer was 'no'. Shankar was not lazy. He was just trying to hustle me. If he could get me to hole up in Tukuche for the night, then he could eat and stay here for free before taking the bus in the morning. *This relationship has to end immediately.*

But I quickly decided this was the wrong place to have our final discussion. The backpacks—and presumably the trekker permits – were outside. Also, to be quite honest, I wanted the discussion to be out in an open space. Shankar did not appear to be a violent person—and I damn sure am not one—but I wanted room for maneuverability if the very worst happened.

"Okay, I go to the bathroom, Shankar," I said. "Then I meet you outside for trekking permits and tip."

He said nothing and I headed off to the bathroom. And when I got outside, there was what could perhaps be called, 'revelation'. The two backpacks were on the bench propped up against the table. But there weren't any trekking permits to be seen. Instead, lying on the table between the two backpacks was a sharp, medium-sized dagger.

***

What the hell do I do, now? Perhaps pull out my Lonely Planet Travel Guide and go to the subtitle – 'What To Do When Your Porter Pulls Out A Large Knife'? Presumably there is a commonsense solution offered. Probably something along the lines of run like hell.

In any event, I tried to act like I didn't notice it. But I thought – I'm not completely sure, but I do think – I saw a small smile purse Shankar's lips. Fortunately, a French girl I had met last night was at the other table outside of the restaurant; I did a beeline to her table to collect my wits. She was immediately 'Chatty Cathy', which helped relieve the tremors of terror that were now surging through my body. But her coquettish ways instantly aroused her porter, who quickly came up from behind and propped his elbows on her shoulders, leering at me as I talked with her. The porter didn't speak a word of English or French; but according to the French girl, he had just carried her through a surging stream after they had somehow ended up on the wrong side of the river. Not only had he saved her, but he also appeared to have been struck through with Cupid's arrow.

"I'm taking the bus two days forward to Tatopani," she told me, "so I have time to do the *ABC trek*. Take the bus with me." My heart sank; her invitation was a great temptation. But there were three strikes against the idea. Shankar would be on the bus, the porter now tethered to this girl would probably be insanely possessive, and, of course, my virtual horror of Nepali buses. I declined. *Maybe I will see her later on the ABC trek.*

Now I simply had to bring closure to my most immediate

problem. I had decided a couple hours ago that I was willing to cough up 4,000 rupees ($50) to prevent the situation with Shankar from becoming far worse. *But he's got a big knife out.* Knives, guns, etc. are so far removed from the way I think, that my composure was almost completely shot.

"Shankar, we now need to make an exchange," I said as he listened intently. "I am going to give you a generous tip. Five-thousand rupees." He frowned at first, probably thinking it was essential to show displeasure. I turned away to break the tension and started chatting with the French girl about the food. I heard Shankar beside me rustling through his belongings. "Bill, here permits." I reached into my money bag, pulled out 5,000 rupees (about $62), and handed it to him without either of us saying a word.

I hated getting ripped off, just as much as anybody else would have. And to be honest, this was really as much about pride and humiliation, as it was about money. But as mentioned before, my every instinct in a situation this fraught with uncertainty is to defuse tensions. If ever there was a time to bolt in anger, without a further word, this was it. But romantic fool that I am, I simply did not like the idea that this was the only thing to remember about someone who, after all, I had been through some intense situations with. Integrity seemed to demand more. Besides, at the time (my doubts have since been completely alleviated) the thing was such a shock, I was only 80% sure that the damn knife was his.

"Shankar," I said looking him in the eye, "You are a good porter, but you need to work on your business skills." A smile again began to purse his lips, but he quickly got control of it. *What is he thinking? That he's a genius who has just created a new business model for Nepali porters to bargain with their clients?* We shook hands and I bolted out of Tukuche.

When I got to the local water station at the edge of town to get the discounted water, it was locked. *Damn, damn.* I had less than one-half liter of water left and there would not be any towns for hours. But the only way I could get water was to go back to the restaurant; and I didn't want to lay my eyes on Mr. Shankar Aryal ever again.

He's going to be bragging to his friends about what he did to shake me down. I'm going to Vijay when I get back to Kathmandu and get the son of a bitch fired. I wonder if I've screwed future trekkers by caving so easily? But probably the most agonizing thought was that my original plan upon arriving in Nepal had been correct—to walk alone until I arrived in Manang and then maybe get one of the many porters that were available there. Of course, that had been my last line of defense against Vijay; but he had turned it into a *Maginot Line* with the esoteric bit about uninsured runaway porters. I simply had not had the courage of my convictions.

In fact, the last laugh probably went not to Shankar, but rather Vijay. Shankar's sharp interrogation about how much I had paid Vijay indicated Vijay had probably low-balled *him*, in addition to high-balling me.

As a final note, upon returning to Kathmandu a couple weeks hence, one of the first places I went was to *Himalayan Scenery Treks and Expeditions, Ltd.*, to see Vijay. I told him exactly what happened.

"Well it's very common for sherpas to carry a knife," he responded with a touch of defensiveness.

"But Vijay, he used that knife to intimidate me and extort a bigger tip than I was planning to give him."

"I will talk to him," Vijay said. Actually, he mainly seemed impressed by the size of the tip I had given Shankar; so he probably *did* talk to him. But then I said, looking him in the eye, "Vijay, I was definitely only going to give Shankar 4,000 rupees. The last 1,000 was extortion. You should pay me 1,000 rupees back."

Vijay could best be classified as a con man, not a crook. He was used to operating subtly. But he immediately began to blush upon my demand. "Shankar has all the money," he said. "There is nothing I can do." *Sure.*

"Okay," I said, closing the conversation, "I am going to go on the internet and talk about what happened."

I walked out. On the way back to the hotel I decided to wait until returning back to America before lambasting his company online, just in case Vijay had some 'Heavies' in his entourage (There were always some unidentified males milling out front of his office. That is often the way the game is played in these parts). When I got back to America, I went online the first day to look for a trekking website. I found one, but—technophobe that I am—could not figure out how to get the message through. Yes, Vijay knew a weak foe when he saw one.

History books are replete with tales of western industrial powers exploiting the people and resources of a country like Nepal. But the denizens from these same large countries have also then traditionally headed off on sojourns of cultural broadening to those same subjugated countries. And many of these wayfarers have similar or even worse tales to report of guile, trickery, and debauchery aimed at them—often successfully. So taking the 'long view', perhaps there is some fair play aspect to my porter experience in Nepal. Perhaps.

BILL WALKER

CHAPTER 18

Freedom

The irony was that I had chosen my first afternoon without a porter to take on the most ambitious hike yet in terms of distance. And now I would be carrying 30 pounds, instead of 13.

However, I was in a stubborn mood. "Too far to Kalopani," Shankar had tried telling me. "Five or six hours." *That knave. I'll show I know more about the damn Annapurna Circuit than he does.* But I hadn't left Tukuche until after 1:00, and the black as pitch night descends by 6:00 in these mountains. I had been on many of these 'beat dark' hikes on the Appalachian and Pacific Crest Trails; in fact, the all-out effort required on them constitutes some of my very fondest memories. But you have to be on your 'A game' on these late afternoon pushes. And you don't want any surprises.

Another irony was that this first afternoon of independence was to be the first time since beginning the Circuit, that it was empty. Many had taken the bus. And Annapurna Circuit trekkers are notorious 'early birds' to begin with; so anybody going all the way to Kalopani today on foot was already well down the road. I was going to be alone. But the brouhaha with Shankar had brought out my competitive spirits. I sure as heck had plenty to think about.

But despite everything, the snowy Dhalagiri and Nilgiri ranges out in the distance, in tandem with the serene river flowing at my side, made me realize I was a lucky man to be right here in Nepal on October 20, 2012, walking the Annapurna Circuit.

The Circuit soon entered a wide riverbed, leaving the afternoon trekker open to clobbering by the wind. But then the trail unexpectedly veered towards a warren of back alleys and houses. I was at a loss for direction, and wandered around scoping various options out. Finally, I spied an elderly Nepali lady.

"Annapurna Circuit," I said in a questioning tone and began pointing in various ways.

"Annapurna," she repeated, before very slowly lowering her entire body and placing the buckets on the ground. She then pointed to the narrow alley to her left. Actually, I found this encounter instructive. For I was to ask countless people in Nepal exactly in which direction the Annapurna Circuit led. And not a single time did the person not know the exact answer, no matter how little English they spoke. They are proud of this Circuit and respect the trekkers who come here from all over the world.

I veered and weaved and turned for the better part of a couple hours, in varying states of assurance. But ultimately the Circuit headed back to the road. Soon I heard a couple buses in the distance and immediately drew up to a more erect posture. *He might be on that damn bus. I want to look like I'm galloping away.*

Late in the afternoon I was following the dirt road when it appeared to go all the way around the mostly dried up river in a horseshoe shape. The road coming back in this direction was only about 200 meters away from where I now stood. However, to get there, I had the choice of picking my way through the soggy river bed or walking about two kilometers around this marsh. Tramping through this mush would save a half-hour – no trivial consideration this time of day. But this seemed like the wrong time and place to risk much of anything. So I opted for the longer route.

But an hour later I was loping up the road when I was suddenly faced with another decision. The longest suspension bridge I had yet seen now came into view. Again, I was gripped by doubt. *I don't want to take that.* And now that I was no longer with the masses I didn't have to face the humiliation of chickening out. I could just stay on the road and would eventually end up in Kalopani. Or at least I thought so. But the sign on the road had an arrow pointing to the *Dhaulagiri Icefall*. Besides, my guidebook said to take this suspension bridge.

Not only would this be my longest crossing—140 meters in span—but the first I would have to do carrying my full backpack. It was virtually unimaginable that anyone would ever survive a fall off one of these bridges. But if you had an 'audience', at least there wouldn't have to be a massive search. I'm not trying to be melodramatic. I never heard of anybody actually falling, although quite a few people quietly indicated their fears. "Just go fast," many people said, half-joking, half serious, about these crossings. That didn't seem like very good advice. But who really knew? I urinated, re-tied my shoes, and swallowed some water, before getting in as low of a crouch as possible. Ninety seconds later I was across and immediately glad I had taken the bridge.

For the trail climbed sharply through 'whispering' forests of cypress and juniper before emptying back out into the wide riverbed. Soon I was in the tiny village of *Kokethanti*. After hearing some human noises, I finally got somebody to sell me a bottle of water at a reasonable price. This gave me the sustenance to get right back going again and beat dark. By the time I got to Kalopani, I felt whole again. *Damn Vijay. He hadn't just taken my money. He had abridged my freedom as well.* The consolation, though, was that now

I really was looking forward to every day of trekking, and doing things my way. It was great to be liberated.

***

Of course, 'my way' is often riddled with mishaps. Wandering the street in Kalopani looking for a place, I ran into the German girl, Greta. "I'm staying back at the first teahouse on the right," she said. "There is hot water." I rushed back. Of course, Vijay had implanted fears in me that if I was by myself, I would have trouble getting rooms and food at affordable prices. Fortunately, that soon proved to be not only a lie, but a damnable one.

The owners saw me to my room and quickly had family members popping in to help me juxtapose the beds in long, diagonal fashion. But I then proceeded to mar the evening, by attempting to take a shower. This was a mistake of simple greed. We were still above 8,000 feet (2,560 meters), with cold, windy weather in the evenings. And I damn well knew that the hot water at these teahouses quickly ran out. But after walking all day, Greta's comment on the hot water had hit a tender spot. The results, given my thin and wasting-away frame, were predictable. I got out of the shower freezing and struggled to regain warmth the rest of the night.

At dinner, my fellow trekkers looked at me like some circus freak, bundled up as I was in jackets, coats, and sweaters. I sat at a separate table in misery. But finally they loaded up the furnace under the table with wood and I was able to join in with everyone. The two Scottish girls, Rhona and Bronwen, were on hand and seemed to be involved in a delicate dance with their own Sherpa. He was a take-control type male, working for two women. His English was good and he kept coming over to give monologues about the food, their exact schedule tomorrow, etc. At first I thought the two Scottish ladies were in his thrall; but knowing the British the way I do, I should have known it was more complicated.

"Can I have some chips?" Bronwen asked him as he was taking their dinner orders. *Did I hear that correctly? Why the hell did she have to ask her porter if she could have some chips?* I would soon learn.

***

Morale was high. I was walking downhill, the morning sunshine was out, and I was warm. At my side was an older German man I had just come up on. He was one of the few people carrying his own backpack, which had immediately made us kindred souls.

"The only reason I can think of that they are carrying our (Westerners') backpacks is because we have more money than they do," he said with great sincerity.

"There's little doubt about that."

However, our morning idyll received a small jolt when we turned a corner in the trail and another suspension bridge over another roaring stream came into view. But I also saw—or in retrospect, would think I had seen—a dirt road that I could follow a few hundred meters around in a horseshoe-shaped bend exactly to where the suspension bridge ended.

"I'm taking the road," I said to the German, which caused him to turn back and give me curious look. Maybe it's just a little weird to be so tall and yet so afraid of height.

Soon I rounded the bend to head back in the direction I had come from; but there were actually two paths. The one to the left had a large puddle and appeared to lead into the river. So I went right, expecting to come up on the dirt road right away. However, I soon found myself deep in the woods. *The mountain to my right is too vertical to possibly go over; so by necessity this path I'm on has to feed back to the Annapurna Circuit down to the left.*

The question of why I didn't just turn back is Freudian in nature. Perhaps it was again a case of simple greed; I had already added some distance by taking the long route around, and didn't want to add any more. Every so often my hopes would get a boost as I peered down through the steep woods and saw some Annapurna trekkers on the road down below. In fact, when you get lost—and I have a long, rich history of doing so—it is only natural to hurry. Soon, in fact, I caught up with the German man I had been with; but of course I couldn't get to where he was 100 meters away. *Or could I?*

The same pattern continued. Occasionally this little rabbit trail veered a a bit downhill, getting my hopes up that it would soon connect to the road. But then my hopes would be dashed again by a rightward turn back up the hill. It was much tougher going up on this steep hillside than their leisurely downhill walk along the river. *Dammit, this was the kind of thing that used to happen to me on the Appalachian and Pacific Crest Trail. But it isn't supposed to on the Annapurna Circuit.* My life wasn't in danger by any means unless I did something really stupid here. I could always turn back; but now that would be a considerable loss of time. A morbid thought began recurring: *what if I am not able to get out of here. Nobody would ever have any clue what happened to me.*

Finally, I came to what appeared to be a dried up waterfall that led down to the road. *This is my chance to get down to that road. But be damn careful.*

I took off my backpack and decided I would try sliding down, putting on the brakes sharply with my two trekking poles. I had approximately 90 meters to descend. The first two slides were well executed, although the sharp jolt I got from stopping reinforced just how steep this whatever-the-hell-you-want-to-call-it was. The third slide, however, is the one that told me I was in quite a pickle. My right trekking pole snapped in two and I skidded right up to a steep precipice. I was now only 20 meters from the road. But had I been able to see from above just how big of a drop-off there was here, I simply wouldn't have tried this. And it was now far too steep to consider scaling back up. As luck would have it, a young Dutchman was toodling by when he heard a ruckus stirring up above him. "I did not know what kind of animal it was," he later recalled with amusement.

"Excuse me," I called down to him, "do you see anywhere for me to land down there?"

"Well," he said half in laughter and half in disbelief, "maybe."

"I'm up here by accident," I said to alleviate any concerns he might have that he was confronting a completely crazy person.

"What happened?" he asked incredulously.

"I missed a turn," I halfway explained.

"Can I help in any way?" he asked.

"Yes," I said. "Can you climb up and let me try to hand you my backpack?"

"I will try."

We both took to all fours; after hesitating in the air for almost half-a-minute, we were able to effect the exchange. "Thanks," I said, "that should make it easier." I chunked my remaining pole down to the road and began slowly to climb down the way this guy had come up. Finally, I was able to jump the last few feet and I was back on the Circuit. Today was supposed to have been a downhill glide cakewalk. Count on me to screw it up; and I was damn lucky this Dutchman had come by at all.

Almost as fortuitous was that Rhona and Bronwen came strolling by at this time.

"My, my, we sure have dirtied ourselves up now, haven't we," Bronwen noted of my entire dirt-covered behind.

"Ya'll are missin' all the fun," I responded. But since they were Scottish, I didn't want to overwhelm them with too theatrical of a description. They told me a little bit about themselves. Rhona was a lawyer in Edinborough, while Bronwen was an up and coming printmaker in artsy Glasgow.

"Who deserves the credit – or blame – for you both being in Nepal?"

"We Brits have a long history here" (Very true. Just consider George Mallary, who when asked why he wanted to ascend Everest, answered, "Because it is there." He probably was the first successful summiteer in 1923, but died on the way down. But the Brits didn't give up there, as the first ten attempts at the Everest summit were by British expeditions), Rhona answered.

"Did you arrange your trekking company back in Scotland?"

"Yes."

"Your guide looks like he's really with it," I observed.

"Well….," they both laughed.

"But I did notice that you asked him for permission to order chips," I said, "and thought, 'what the hell'?"

That observation immediately set them off on their own tale of porter turbulence. It seems that their capable and energetic guide was also a bit headstrong. One day he had apparently led them on a completely different schedule than they had anticipated, which drew their ire.

"We almost sacked him," Bronwen said, using British parlance for firing.

"But how do you sack someone out here in the middle of nowhere?" I asked. Of course, it was a question I had been grappling with myself.

"I don't know but there must be some way to do it," the lawyer, Rhona, said.

They had more faith than me that they had at least some rights and would not be completely screwed. Perhaps it was because they had a more reputable trekking company. But their arrangement was a bit unusual in that they had one guy doubling as a porter and guide. He came off as strong, energetic, and determined. "I want my own trekking company," he stated in a display of American-style ambition, and repeatedly questioned me about my home country. But at the end of the day, he was a Nepali male. Like most males in developing countries, they simply have trouble engaging in lateral relationships with females.

And to think that last night I had thought this guide-porter was being possessive while I was chatting to his two clients. Perhaps that says as much about me, as it does about the bloody porter!

BILL WALKER

CHAPTER 19

Downhill

"Why in the hell anybody would even consider taking a bus is beyond me," I chortled to Rhona and Bronwen.

"We had no trouble deciding to give it a miss," Rhona said.

"Honestly though, a bus is much more dangerous here than walking," I continued haranguing. But the damn truth really was that the margin of error for the buses going down these narrow mountain roads was horrifyingly narrow. One tilt to the left and the bus would be gone for several hundred feet. Perhaps it's just human to want to do 'the easy thing'. But to do it in the Himalayas, and specifically right here, was especially unfortunate.

For we found ourselves—surprisingly—in the midst of some of the most dramatic scenery since beginning the Circuit. In fact, this gorge along the Kali Gandaki River that we were descending through to inexorably low elevations, is the *largest gorge in the world*. The reason for such a cavernous geographic formation is actually pretty simple. The summits of two of the largest mountains in the world – Dhaulagiri and Annapurna I, both over 26,000 feet (8,000 meters) – stand just miles from each other. The river, which had been flowing in our direction for a couple days now, narrowed to a thundering torrent as it cut between the mountains through the gorge. I absolutely loved it.

*Deep gorges between towering mountains
are a daily feature of the Annapurna experience*

When the two girls stopped to use the bathroom in the bushes, I continued on. But my momentum was once again abridged by my old bugaboo, a suspension bridge. And this wasn't any old bridge either, but a rickety metal and wood apparatus dangling 475 feet (150 meters) across a surging waterway down below. *I may not try this.* However, the trail on the other side of the river looked like it was rolling through some especially fetching country that I definitely wanted to be part of. And besides, Rhona and Bronwen would surely cross this bridge with dispatch. So I slowly began to edge my way across.

Immediately I felt more uncomfortable than I had felt yet on one of these swinging contraptions. And this time I wasn't just uncomfortable, but outright scared. *Maybe I should try crawling?* Crawling? I had often thought about adopting such a coping mechanism when confronted with these swinging contraptions.

But with 30 pounds on my back, I would only become more wobbly. *Okay, that settles it. I'm not doing this. I'm turning around and taking the road.*

I turned around and started tiptoeing in the opposite direction when I heard a familiar voice. "Bill, is there a problem with the bridge?" Rhona and Bronwen approached with quizzical looks.

"No, ya'll just go ahead," I quickly said. "I'm just gonna' wait until you're both over. I don't want the bridge swinging, while I'm crossing."

"Oh, okay."

Fortunately, Scots are long on tact and didn't taunt me. But suddenly retreat no longer seemed like the viable option it had been just 15 seconds before. It simply would have been too humiliating to do in front of these two attractive ladies – just another chapter in the long, tortured male history of *'Follow Your Ego'*.

"Wow, this is a long one," Bronwen commented as they dutifully strolled past me. At least they showed enough respect to not lean halfway over the rail like some trekkers and start snapping photos. Once over, they stood and waited for me. For the second time I started across.

There is no reason to be melodramatic. What I was doing was really very ordinary. Actually, the biggest danger may have been an overactive imagination. But heck, a person naturally feels small and inconsequential when surrounded by towering mountains and powerful waterways. It didn't exactly require a Robert Louis Stevenson to conjure up a horror scenario with a 150 foot dropoff.

Again, I concentrated on maintaining as low of a center of gravity as I could sustain. *Am I halfway yet?* Every time I crossed a suspension bridge, I was always asking myself that question as I progressed across. Usually I wasn't. But once I got past that point and got closer to the far shore, I began to wonder at what point I could fall and still survive.

"Are you afraid of heights?" Bronwen asked casually, once I arrived at the far shore.

"Take a wild guess."

"What would be the origin of such a phobia?"

"Well, let me just give you the analysis of my ex-girlfriend in Chicago," I offered. "She lived in a high-rise in downtown Chicago. When we went up to her rooftop, I was always petrified about getting anywhere near the edge. It so happens that at around that same time I was having problems with both insomnia, as well as making a commitment to this particular girl. Ultimately, all of this led her to develop what you might call a unified field theory about me. 'Bill, you're scared of heights, scared of falling asleep, and scared of falling in love'."

That drew a laugh, if a dubious one, out of them. But perhaps it helped build camaraderie as we traipsed through the wilderness. This section was especially scenic. The trail climbed up a steep, rocky incline, and then maintained a high elevation on the cliff above the river, coursing sharply through forests of pine, cypress, and juniper. We finally arrived at some steep stone steps, which we followed down to the tiny hillside village of *Pairothapla*. There a group of approximately twenty trekkers speaking a foreign tongue were milling about the general store.

"German?" I asked.

"Yes," one fortyish woman replied.

"And why have I met more Austrians than Germans?" That drew sighs from a few of them, before one answered, "They have more time on their hands." Perhaps that is true; however, the name 'Reinhold Messner' comes to mind. This Austrian alpinist is widely considered considered to be the greatest mountaineer of all time. And needless to say, his greatest exploits occurred in this magnificent mountain chain, the Himalayas.

"And yourself?" the lady asked me. "Where are you from?"

"United States." Given the worldwide revulsion directed against *Uncle Sam* in the last decade, I've learned to be on guard when giving this answer (although I've never taken the time-honored dodge of telling people I'm Canadian). However, Germans never have fallen full-fledged into this cheap brand of anti-American mockery, probably because of their own historical legacy. In fact, from what I've seen Germans are held to a higher standard than other travelers while overseas. Better yet, they usually meet it, whether it be in languages, preparation, etiquette, or whatever. But given the stigma still attached to their nationality, they are often shy to come forward and introduce themselves.

"What city are you from?"

"All over," one volunteered, and suddenly they all wanted to chat, perhaps because most of their social interaction up to this point had been confined to their fellow Germans. Of course, the British are habitually quite distant when around Germans (for reasons I don't need to explain), and Rhona and Bronwen were no different.

"Are you ready Bill?" Rhona asked. "There's a bridge down here at the bottom." *That* piece of news quickly ended my idle chat with the Germans. I did a Harold Holt bolt with Bronwen and Rhona right out of this small village to beat this big crowd of Germans, so there wouldn't be ten of us on the bridge at one time.

One problem with paranoias is that they simply become boring after a while. I decided it was time to 'zip it' about suspension bridges, and just get on with it. This second bridge was also a substantial span. But we made it over without incident, and now luxuriated in a downhill glide on the main road. Soon we came upon a waterfall streaming down the face of the mountain in countless rivulets, before finally spilling out onto the road. Jeeps splashed their way through the falls and we were able to easily tiptoe through it. But it didn't take an expert mountaineer to see that in rainy season, or anything resembling it for that matter, this section would have been flat-out impassable.

Rhona and Bronwen
These two Scots never seemed far off kilter

"Hey, let's get in the waterfall," Bronwen said. However, my appetite for adventure was flagging. Rhona and I stood there while Bronwen reveled at the foot of the cascades. Soon we headed down the hill where we found a restaurant within clear view of the falls. Life didn't suck.

"Can we have some chips?" Rhona, the lawyer, again asked their guide, who went in to order them. This lawyer-artist tandem had a breezy confidence about them that seemed to have reined their porter in. After my own abysmal ending with my own porter, I looked on enviously.

We took our time eating and drinking before winding the last few kilometers down to Tatopani. Since clearing Thorung La Pass three-and-a-half days ago, we had descended a whopping 14,000 feet. The honest-to-God truth is that there really are not many places in the world that an average person gets to do something that outright cool. We were now below 4,000 feet; not only was I able to take off the bundles of clothing I had worn each night, but suddenly everything looked and even smelled differently. That evening we basked in the plush greenery and fragrant tropical delights of the *Dhaulagiri Lodge.*

I had greatly enjoyed Rhona and Bronwen's company. But they were on a tight schedule and headed straight to the finish line, and then on to Scotland. However, I was carrying a full backpack. That had barely held me back at all on the huge descent of the last few days. Now, though, we would be headed back up big-time, climbing straight out of here The stark fact was that I would not be able to maintain the same pace as these two lasses going uphill. So I bid the two fair-feathered ladies farewell and would miss their wry senses of humor.

BILL WALKER

CHAPTER 20

Annapurna Ending and Beginning

There simply are not many places in the world a person such as myself can ascend 5,000 feet in one day. But having given up huge amounts of elevation in such a short time, it was inevitable that we would go back up. In fact, the climb out of Tatopani would be the longest single day climb I've ever done.

The ascent was stiff and unrelenting. We climbed up long flights of stone steps, perspiring in the sub-tropical heat. I was fortunate to have hooked up with a Dutch couple in their mid-twenties, along with a young mountain lion from the Dolomites region in the Italian Alps. Perhaps there is just something about 5,000 foot climbs that breeds camaraderie, for we had bonded instantly. I found it endearing that none of them had ever used any guides or porters.

The twosome from Holland went about things in a typically spare Dutch manner, while the Italian provided the special brand of flair found in that Mediterranean peninsula. I was psyched up just trying to maintain their pace. We made good progress. Every half hour we would look back down and see how much further we had gotten from the gorge and rushing water, which only boosted morale further. Finally, after ascending 3,000 feet, we arrived in the village of *Sikha*, and stopped for lunch.

"*Dhal bat,*" the Dutchmen, Willums, immediately said to the waiter, referencing the national dish of lentil soup and rice curry. His girlfriend, Dannika, and the Italian both quickly followed suit. I had watched porters and guides eat Dhal bat twice daily, usually with their hands. While it contained no meat, it was packed with carbs, and restaurants always offered you second helpings. In other words, it was perfect for trekkers.

Dannika was a doctor and Willums was an architect. But they had put their careers on hold and embarked on a six-month journey from Holland, first through Mongolia and western China on bicycle, now all over Nepal, and eventually on to India. In a sense, this is the European way. "Hopefully, we will be able to avoid having to take public assistance," Dannika said matter-of-factly.

Lingering wasn't their style, either. They ate with dispatch and prepared to ascend further, forcing me to hurry through lunch to stay with them. As we neared Ghorepani in the late afternoon, we passed by a relatively modern-looking building bearing a simple sign, HEALTH CLINIC. My guidebook showed that a Flemish Belgian man named Paul Moortel had arranged its construction. And, lo and behold, when I popped my head in the clinic to ask if Moortel ever visited, a non-descript, middle-aged man replied, "That is me." Indeed he was quite happy to talk all about all his varied activities in Nepal. Being a curious soul, I stuck around to chat, while my companions headed on to get fixed up for the evening.

"How did you decide to build the clinic?" I asked.

"I married a girl from the village," he replied. "See that lady right there," he motioned over at a Nepali lady, "that's her sister."

"Do you live here?" I asked.

"I've been coming to Nepal six months a year for twenty years."

Six months a year for twenty years. That tells you something about what this strange, exotic land does to foreigners.

"Where does the money come from to fund the clinic?"

"I raise the money in Belgium," he quickly answered, "We also built a school here in the village."

It should be said, Moortel was not just another 'do-gooder'. Nepali after Nepali had surprised us with tales of never having attended formal school. I continued to be staggered by porters and guides I had been walking along with for days, only to hear them answer matter-of-factly that they had never attended a single day of school (Shankar told me he had about two years of formal schooling). And up here in these highlands, there is an especially desperate need for health clinics and schools. The good news is that the oft-maligned international NGO's (non-governmental organizations) really are starting to have an impact.

Unsurprisingly, Moortel was a bit of a storyteller. "You think the stories you read in the news about the people killed in avalanches and bus crashes are bad," he said, "then you should listen to the ones I hear about that never get reported." He then went into yet another rant (I had already heard several complaints from guides and porters) about Israeli trekkers, which I took as my cue to cut away. I hurried out the door in order to make it to Ghorepani before dark.

***

The thinning air again took on a nip as the trail made a final ascent through forests of rhododendron, birch and magnolia. Finally, I arrived in the hilltop town of Ghorepani. At the risk of overromanticizing it, Ghorepani, in a certain way, is to Nepal what the hilltop town of Assisi is to Italy. It became a trendy destination back in the 1960's and has seen its share of famous visitors, including Muhammed Ali, Jimmy Hendrix, Pele, and yes, Tenzig Norgay (who is the most famous Nepali ever, despite having lived most of his life in India). The breathtaking panorama of snow-covered peaks that is immediately presented gives ample reason why.

A flourish of pride swelled up in me at my 5,000 foot day. The majority of trekkers continue right on over this hill and descend a steep 5,000 feet to *Birethanti*, which marks the end of the Annapurna Circuit. From there they catch the bus to *Pokhara*, which lies at the foot of the mountains. Most people were openly craving the renowned spas, cuisine, and water sports that lay in Pokhara. And I was certainly no different. From my past treks, I knew the wasting away-effect that mountains and cold weather have on my lean frame. Indeed, Pokhara sounded like *Shangri-La*.

But I hadn't come from the other side of the world to bask in the comforts of a resort town. I was here to experience the Himalayas – agonies, ecstasies, and all. Up until now they certainly had lived up to their billing, and I wanted to get more of them. Given the seemingly infinite possibilities, the question was where to go from here.

I had been studying the guidebook closely and questioning experienced trekkers. It soon became very clear that there was, in fact, a second very popular trek in Nepal – the *Annapurna Base Camp (ABC)* trek in the Annapurna Sanctuary.

CHAPTER 21

Here Come the Chinese

"Who are all these people?" Dannika asked in wonderment.

"The character of the trek has changed," Willums lamented.

But I just kept my mouth shut. Because, in reality, I was a bit psyched up at what I was seeing.

The Himalayas routinely dole out 'eye candy' the likes of which the average mortal doesn't get in a lifetime

It was the day after the big ascent. I had followed my map, which showed that I could go directly east out of Ghorepani and within two days I would join up with the Annapurna Base Camp trek. Better yet was the terrain on this route – it actually went both up *and* down (Flat apparently does not exist in Nepal).

After ascending steeply out of Ghorepani this morning, I had gotten back above 10,000 feet.

Crowds had been gathered at the top of the hill around a monument with their cameras out. White-capped mountains extending from the Annapurna, Dhaulagiri, and Machhapuchhre ranges extended as far as the eye can see. By my lights, this particular spot was the most underrated view in the entire Annapurna range.

The other big surprise was the number of people. Amazingly, there were even more people than there had been on the Circuit. It seems that hordes of 'tourists' opt for the shorter ABC trek over the Annapurna Circuit. They begin in Nepal's second city of Pokhara and ascend through here (just as Arlene Blum's historic woman's expedition had in 1978 on the way to the Annapurna Base Camp).

Leaving this hilltop, I had reveled in building up a healthy sweat along the series of ups and downs that are the normal fare of long-distance hiking. After hours of following a narrow stream and passing large groups of theretofore unseen hikers, I had stopped for a quick lunch of *Dhal Bat* in Banthanti. It was when I had gotten to my day's intended destination, *Tadapani,* the confusion had surfaced.

Scores – make it hundreds – of people were rushing all over the village. I had no idea where to even begin looking for a place to stay. When I tried walking into the teahouses to inquire about a room, it was impossible to tell just who to talk to about getting a room. Finally, I had run into Dannika and Willums. The mob scene here in this village clearly didn't fit their understated styles.

The demographic character of the trek appeared to have changed dramatically. In place of predominantly Europeans, there were now more Asians. "I think they're Chinese," Willums answered Dannika's query about the nationality of the 'new' trekkers.

That was cool with me. Heck, it had actually been a bit embarrassing that up until now I had only come across a handful of trekkers from Nepal (Imagine a foreigner going over to hike the

Appalachian Trail, only to spot just a few Americans on the trail). Obviously, this was for reason of basic economics. But China was right next door; it was logical that they would be here in large numbers. Apparently Chinese trekkers prefer the shorter *ABC* trek over the more extended Annapurna Circuit. This was also a matter of economics.

"The Chinese are finally doing trekking," a Nepali guide later told me. "They just don't spend much money." But then he had gone on to voice the standard harsh Nepali criticism of the Indians ("They won't trek. All they want to do is stay in our cities and make money.").

"I don't think I'm going to stay here," I said to Dannika and Willums, even though it was late afternoon. "Something just tells me to go."

***

The trail itself was now abandoned. But the forests were dark and full of life. Small volts of tension rippled through me.

Suddenly I heard some larger animals rifling through a nearby tree and stood there at rapt attention. I couldn't believe my eyes. I was looking at a bunch of monkeys. "Monkeys?" people replied in disbelief the next day when I told them about it. But my guidebook did indeed indicate that this particular forest was sometimes alive with herds of so-called *langur monkeys*. After a few minutes, I walked away with a greater awareness of the derivation of the phrase, "more fun than a barrel of monkeys," as they heaved up and down with unfeigned ecstasy.

The trail continued winding down a mountain through the dense forest. *At least it should be a bit warmer tonight.* I was hoping to get to the *Panorama Point Lodge*. An hour later the trail spit me out of the woods and onto the wide lawn of a handsome, two-story hotel with a commanding view of the distant mountains and gorge below. *Cool. I'll stay here.*

However, when I finally found the right person to talk to amongst the large crowd assembled, I was told this place was full. This meant continuing on a steep descent towards the river, with nighttime now beginning to threaten. My guidebook mentioned an old British Gurkha lodge that was on this steep bank somewhere between here and the river. At the very least, this sounded like an intriguing option. But given their legendary reputation – the Gurkhas of Nepal have long been ranked among the most valiant fighting forces in history – I wondered if the lodge might be booked months in advance. Finally at dusk, I was relieved to come upon a lone, spare-looking lodge at the last ledge before the river.

A young girl – maybe 16 or 17, and approximately four-and-a-half feet tall – who later told me she had never even ventured past the nearby village, nor attended a single day of school, showed me a room. The only other trekker staying here was a Norwegian girl who was headed in the opposite direction tomorrow. I was glad I had trekked until dark, because there was not a thing to do here other than eat and go to sleep in my cold room. The Gurkhas never had it so tough!

***

Like many westerners, I have found Asians to be inscrutable at times (Note: They surely find us just as mystifying). But the great thing about long-distance hiking is that 'masks' get removed and reality is revealed.

Dannika and Willums had blown Tadapani at first light and quickly caught up with me. Americans, Europeans, and Asians alike – we were all bending deeply into the mountain, struggling, panting, suddenly pulling over for breaks, then forcing ourselves to continue. Nationality tends to give way to human realities. I saw one group of Asians making fun of a bespectacled hiker who began screaming irately back at them. My mind went back to a Chinese pilgrim that I had witnessed on El Camino de Santiago. After a big descent, the poor fella' realized he had left his camera on top of the mountain. He had quickly dropped his backpack and begun wildly stabbing the air with his trekking poles as he retraced his steps back up the mountain. These are all emotions that I can personally identify with, and often find endearing.

By the time we arrived in Chomrong, we were being pelted by cold rain drops. My appetite for a new ascent was also beginning to flag. *You've already completed the trek you came to Nepal for. You don't have any pressure to go to Annapurna Base Camp. It's going to be cold as hell up there, and you're going to be miserable.* Once again, I was in 'Hamlet mode'.

But ultimately the decisive factor proved to be what country I was in. This was a once-in-a-lifetime trip; I probably wasn't ever going to return to Nepal, if for no other reason than my phobia of suspension bridges. So the overriding imperative was to do all the trekking I wanted to do right now. With that in mind, I trailed Dannika and Willums out of Chomrung.

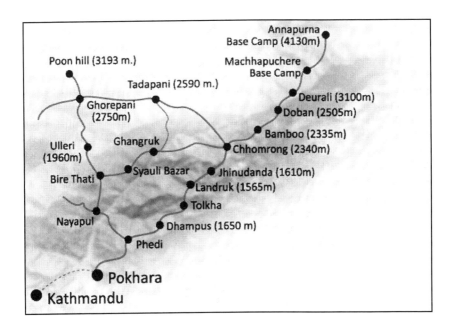

Chapter 22

ABC

The Annapurna Base Camp trek (ABC) takes you right into the heart of the Annapurna range in a way that the Annapurna Circuit does not. While it does not go as high as the Circuit (13,550 feet, compared to 17,768 feet), it is considered more difficult step-for-step. The grades are steeper which, of course, meant acclimatization would be more difficult.

I got a taste of that right away with a steep descent down to the *Modi Khola Canyon*, crossing a suspension bridge over a tributary stream, and then a grueling late-afternoon climb up stone steps at a 45 degree angle to the small village of *Sinuwa*. Dannika and Willums had predictably made it up the hill faster than me and gotten the last room in the big lodge. Clusters of French that I had met earlier on the Circuit hovered around.

Damn me for being so sentimental, (*perhaps because I come from a family and country of French haters*), but I just couldn't get over the way their smiles all seemed to come from the diaphragm. They really seemed glad to see me. A few of them even went scurrying around scoping out various options for me to sleep in dining rooms, etc. But ultimately I decided to stay at the smaller lodge 100 meters away.

Three women from California who had just descended from ABC were there, and they proceeded to put a damper on my evening. "It was slick and dangerous coming down from there," one lady said emphatically. "You aren't wearing those shoes up there, are you?" *My damn shoes. Here goes that issue again.* But there was another big issue – the crowds of people.

"The teahouses are all fully booked," all of them said with certitude. "If your guide or trekking company does not have a reservation, you will probably not be able to get a place to stay."

Heck, *that* probably would have concerned even a more confident trekker. But I actually found a bit of relief in it for a very simple reason: I was looking for an excuse to bow out of heading up to ABC. (Please note: this narrative is not a 'how to' book. In fact, one reason I got into writing outdoor narratives is because I got tired of reading books written by experts for other experts in a narrow expert's language).

So for the second time since arriving in the Himalayas, I went to bed not sure if I was going to be ascending or descending the next day. It simply was not that important to my trip in Nepal; and I was dreading being miserable at the high altitude for a few more days. *I'll decide in the morning.*

We were still only at 7,300 feet (2,340 meters), and I was able to get a decent night's sleep. That was critical; I knew from past experience it was unlikely to be repeated higher up. But I had also looked closely at the map and decided that I might just be able to get to *ABC* in two days, and then back down to here on a third night. So I would only be 'on the clock' for three days and two nights. That gave me encouragement to go forward. But first I did something uncharacteristic.

When I went in to pay my bill, I asked the owner of the teahouse if he would call and get me a reservation in *Deurali* for tonight. My guidebook listed it as a two-day trek from here; but like most guidebooks it probably erred on the conservative side. If I hustled, I thought I could make it there in one. In a calm, Nepali mountain way, the owner placed the call. He soon hung up and nodded his head.

"I have a reservation in Deurali tonight?" I confirmed.

"Yes," he said quietly. I have always been critical of people over-planning outdoor trips. But this was one bow to convention that would end up being key.

I began winding my way as fast as I could through dense forests, and was quickly struck by the more jagged nature of this terrain. However, just as in the case of the Circuit, we found ourselves in a gorge between towering peaks with torrid currents rushing down through the valley.

I needed to make it through four 'villages' today, which meant gaining over 3,000 feet in elevation – not exactly what the acclimatization doctor ordered. I say villages; in reality, there were not any villages, towns, or otherwise permanent settlements on this ABC trek. None. The guidebook made it clear these were simply clusters of teahouses for trekkers in the otherwise pristine Himalayas.

***

Speaking of beautiful, when I passed through a dense bamboo jungle and descended steeply down some stone steps, I entered a cluster of lodges appropriately named *Bamboo*. It was a basically a terrace of concrete with four lodges on the periphery. Sitting there having a morning tea was a lithe, Caucasian girl that I had seen on the trail yesterday. Unsurprisingly, she had been surrounded by guys vying for her attention. Not wanting to be a part of any 'wolfpack', I had continued on.

"Good morning," she greeted me, in what sounded like the Queen's English.

"Australian?" I asked.

"Close," she said.

"Oh, you're the real thing."

"Well yes, so to say. But I now live in Australia."

I've gotta' admit, there is nothing quite like a correct English accent – especially when they're having a cup of tea. In fact, it had always amazed me while living in London for over four years just how excited the British can get over a hot drink. You can just feel it in their more resilient, but ever-correct intonations.

"How do you like Australia?"

"I must say, I quite like it," she said. "My name is Martha, by the way," at which point she proferred her hand.

"Bill, here," I answered. "Yeah, when I was in England, it seemed like everybody's dream was to spend two years in Australia."

"Well, I hope to be there a good bit longer than that."

"You must be attracted to the outdoor life?"

"Oh, I tried working office jobs, and finally decided no more. I work on a sheep farm and am much happier carrying loads around."

"Well then Nepal is the place for you."

"You might say," she laughed.

How in the world does Martha keep her spare frame warm? She had a mere shawl thrown over her outer layer of clothing. So far she was checking all the boxes of the kind of iconoclastic female you would expect to find trekking alone in Nepal. But I would quickly see that she was not of the trendy or flighty variety, but rather a real, dyed-in-the-wool trekker. Martha and I set off together into the dark, thick forest.

We continued crossing surging streams over rickety wooden

bridges. With all the rushing water and jungle-like terrain, I shouldn't have been surprised when we came to a large cascading waterfall(s). This exact location alone was said to diverge into over 100 channels of crashing water during the rainy season (No wonder there were no permanent villages in this immediate area).

However our guidebook repeatedly warned of landslides and avalanches, especially the higher up we got. It didn't take great imagination to conjure up horrors with such steep ravines and plentiful precipitation. I've personally never given much consideration to avalanches when in snowy areas; it had always seemed like luck of the draw, as well as extremely improbable. But there was just something about the Himalayas – and not just their height, but more the angles of the mountains. In fact, the week before I had left for Nepal, nine French and German climbers had been buried alive in avalanches at 20,000 feet.

At mid-day, Martha and I arrived in the lodge cluster of *Himalaya*, where crowds of trekkers, speaking a babble of languages, sat around dining tables. Most seemed relaxed and I got the impression that a lot of them were staying here. *Maybe I should stay here.*

We joined an Australian lady at a crowded table. After she got her anti-American venting out of the way ("I have no interest in ever even visiting such a country." *Gee thanks for letting me know),* she proved to be delightful company. She had made it to *ABC* yesterday and was now headed back.

"Was it bad up there?" I asked.

"No, you shouldn't have any problem," she assured me. "But it's bloody cold. And it gets outrageously slippery towards the top." *No problem, huh?* In fact, most of these people seemed to be on the way down from the top. They were home-free and you could read it in their body language.

My mind kept going back to when I had made the reservations for Nepal. I had chosen to come in October, which is ideal in so many ways (Nepal has the latitude of northern Florida). The monsoon season has ended and trekkers delight in crisp, clear skies. But now we were nearing the end of the month and it had palpably begun to get colder. In fact, if I had known I was going to do two treks while here, instead of just the one I had originally planned on, I would have made my reservations for a couple weeks earlier. But of course, that's all just negative thinking. Martha didn't seem afflicted with such doubts. However, my extensive hiking experience had taught me that you never really knew what was going on in other trekker's minds.

In mid-afternoon, we finally made it to the fourth cluster of lodges known as *Deurali,* having picked up 3,000 feet in elevation for the day. Trekkers were milling around the front doors of the teahouses, which made me wonder if my reservation was solid. *I will go back down if they tell me I have no room. It would be dangerous to go any higher today.*

"This does not look promising," I said to Martha, who had no reservation. Palpably grim looks were drawn across the faces of some trekkers.

"They are full," a German man said.

"So what are you going to do?"

"We have to keep going to *MBC.*"

Wow, I actually out-prepared a German! But actually, I had empathy for their predicament. Now they were going to have ascend another 1,400 feet on top of what they had already done today. Yeah, they had time. But in addition to the shock of such a sharp increase in elevation, MBC would be much colder yet. My heart went out to this group as they began doggedly trudging upward along a barren ridge.

I approached and gave the man my name.

"Oh yes, the tall man," he immediately exclaimed.

Well, I'll be damned. He led me to my room which had three beds in it. After he walked away, I whispered to Martha, "Hey, I'm going to put two beds together. You can have the third one." She threw her things on the third bed, a cool customer about such vicissitudes.

Of course, getting a room didn't solve the problem of staying warm, by any imagination. For starters, you simply don't stay warm at these elevations. Rather, you just sit there huddled up, protecting your body core from becoming hypothermic. As we had customarily done on the Annapurna Circuit, all the trekkers gathered in the dining hall to hunker down and share our body heat. However, there would be no burning stove now that we had cleared tree line.

"I'm knackered," Martha pronounced after about a half-hour of 'teahouse talk'. She headed out and disappeared into the room. A few different times I went back to the room in order to retrieve more clothing. But miraculously, she lay face down on her bed with one blanket thrown over her (she did not own a sleeping bag – the only such trekker, porter, or guide that I saw like that in Nepal) for the better part of 16 hours. *As long as she doesn't die, this will be a huge advantage for her tomorrow.*

***

"I actually slept pretty good," Martha casually remarked first thing in the morning. "And I think I was at it awhile." She quickly downed some porridge and turned it on up the mountain before I could even get things sorted out.

Meanwhile, I was a combination of fatigued and chilled, having lain awake shivering for several hours. But I was still pumped up. Today was all about adrenaline – and uncertainty. There were two potential destinations today. The first was MBC (*Machhapuchhre Base Camp*), a 1,400 foot elevation gain from here. "It's very nice, but cold," trekker after trekker had told me. "But it might be full." Of course, the second and final destination was *ABC – the Annapurna Base Camp* ("Beautiful first thing in the morning, if you can stand the cold. Forget sleeping."), which was another 1,400 feet higher beyond MBC. Actually, the map listed another cluster of lodges strategically located between here and MBC, at *Bagar*. But last night we were told that the Himalayan Rescue Association had forced the owners to abandon them because of avalanches.

And for whatever reason, the minute I began ascending this morning I started thinking this looked like avalanche country. Walls of snow hung above at virtual right angles, with us walking in gullies down below. Actually, from what I had read, avalanches happen all the time. In fact, a half hour after beginning I was walking along when I heard what sounded like a mountain site being dynamited and looked up on the hill to my left. Ripples of snow were tumbling down the steep banks, stopping well short of me. Like most avalanches, it was not in the least deadly.

Once again, I was hurrying – another violation of high altitude etiquette. Honestly though, it wasn't completely irrational. Hordes of trekkers were quite obviously racing, hoping to secure a room tonight at either *MBC* or *ABC*.

The trail ran alongside the thundering river. The colossal white eminences of Annapurna I to the west and Machhapuchhre towerered to our sides, all creating the sensation of a Himalayan wonderland. *Yeah, mountain climbers can be a bit demented. But if I had it in me to get all the way to the summit of one of these huge peaks, I'd probably give it a shot also.* As it was, there was plenty to think about down here as we crossed through several so-called 'avalanche chutes', so named because of their potential to funnel masses of snow downward.

After a couple hours of steady ascent, some handsome looking stone buildings came into view. I came to a final icy bridge before entering *MBC*. Wisely (if I may say so, myself), I got down on my knees and crossed. Falling into freezing cold water at these elevations would have been a flat-out life-endangering proposition.

It was a beautiful, but crispy cold, sunny day. My mood, if not exactly matching the weather, was sturdy. Martha was the first person I saw, sitting on the terrace having a tea.

"Bill, how did you make out?"

"It was generally smooth until I had to take to my knees to get over that icy bridge."

"What icy bridge?"

"The one just down there."

"Oh," she said nonchalantly.

"Are there any places to stay here?" I asked.

"I must tell you," she answered, "I lucked out. A roomful of guys had an extra bed. I asked if I could stay in it and they told me 'yes'."

"So does that mean there aren't any more rooms?"

"I believe not."

"Oh, wow," I muttered. "I don't believe I can stay at *ABC*."

"I'm headed up to *ABC* now, and then coming back down," she said. "Would you like to go?"

"I can feel a migraine coming on. I've got to take a break." And then I added, "The snow is getting heavier. I honestly don't know if it's smart for me to go all the way up with these shoes."

"Okay," she said and got up to head off. Good for her. She obviously knew a loser when she spotted one!

BILL WALKER

CHAPTER 23

ABC?

The human body needs to be pampered at these elevations, not hurried. But with such a short distance remaining, a headache – even a migraine headache – should be a superfluous factor. I purchased another 300 rupee bottle of filtered water and chugged away, attempting to stanch my headache. But that was impossible as it predictably flowered into a full-fledged migraine.

I'll just walk a few hundred meters and test the waters. Of course, I also harbored another thought. *I'm only an hour-and-a-half from the finish of the ABC trek.* I started up.

The snow was of imminent importance. Every step forward was bringing greater depth. And like everybody else out here, I had become an enthusiastic amateur weather forecaster. The pattern that normally prevailed was crystal clear mornings, followed by clouds swooping in during the afternoon. But on days when you did have some clouds in the morning, they almost always turned to precipitation in the afternoon. Today the sun was increasingly being blocked by low-hanging clouds. *It's going to snow. Big deal, right? You're in the Himalayas. Deal with it or get the hell out of here.*

It was entirely predictable that I would hurry. But the strange thing was I really didn't know what I was hurrying for because I wasn't planning to go to the top. Well okay, I wanted to catch up with Martha. She was now just in front of me, with no backpack. Actually, the only decent piece of equipment she seemed to have was a pair of mountaineering boots. *I can't go to the top with these shoes. My socks will be soaked through and I will get hypothermic.*

"Martha," I yelled up ahead, "how much further do you reckon to *ABC*?"

"A half-hour tops," she said.

I soon caught up with her, which was both a good and bad thing. I had maxed out from the opening this morning. Now – predictably – I was predictably feeling the first hints of 'the wall'. *What folly this all is? Turn around.*

"This snow is getting deeper," Martha noted, looking down at my low-cuts.

"Yeah, I'm turning around."

But I didn't want to leave quite yet. And not just because of Martha, either. Trekker's honor. This area we were in right here in the vortex of the Himalayas was getting more dramatic by the moment. A magical Himalayan winterland of soaring, snow-clad mountain ranges in all directions. It really is an amazing fact that eight of the top ten peaks in the world lie within the borders of this relatively small country. And the fact that humans so often move heaven and earth, and risk life and limb, to get to the top of these great mountains shows that we are fundamentally an aspirational species.

"Ah, that must be *ABC*," Martha said when we cleared a long ridge.

Indeed, a modest-sized stone building stood about 500 meters up a modest hill.

"Looks a bit forlorn," Martha observed with a hint of laughter.

Yeah, I would like to get there. But the truth is that the main reason is to just be able to say I've completed the ABC trek. I wasn't going to see much more than I already have. And now I was getting dizzy from having walked too fast, and would soon be flirting with hypothermia because my extremities were getting wet.

Now I was within 300 meters of the building. But they say it's in the journey, not the destination. Or at least that's the motto of us weaklings and cowards.

"Hey, this is enough for me."

"Oh okay," Martha said looking surprised. "Safe travels." The great thing about the British is the way they avoid overwrought goodbyes. I turned around and headed back as fast as I could. Needless to say, ascending trekkers were looking at me with various quizzical expressions. "Have you already been to the top?" a couple people asked. My response was to tactically grunt. But for the most part, this was a pretty cool group of customers. Trekking in the Himalayas is all about vicissitudes and playing the game the best you can. The surprising thing to me while descending was just how far I had actually ascended, given that I had left *MBC* with the ostensible purpose of just checking out the first hilltop. Adrenaline had carried me all morning. But now I was spent.

It took me almost an hour to get back down to *MBC*; the morning flurries had morphed into a full-fledged snow. The worrisome thing, though, was that I had felt better on seemingly every step headed down from Thorung La Pass. But that was not happening here.

The minute I got back to *MBC*, I ordered vegetable fried rice and more water. I then lay there with my head in my arms, wondering if I even had the ability to descend to lower elevations. When the food came I hurried to eat a few bites. But that was all I could handle – another clear sign of at least minor altitude sickness. Yeah, it was bound to be tough up here, in any event. But by maxing out all morning, I had gotten myself in a pickle.

Perversely, my hopes lay in getting back to *Deurali* where I had started the day, and trying to get a room there. But if I couldn't get a room there, well…. As is my wont, I said a quick prayer for faith and again hurried out of *MBC* – but this time to go down.

*****

I did not think anybody else would try to make it up here today. But the impressive thing was that as I started down, I ran into scattered groups of people still ascending – trekkers of obviously average ilk, yet who were taking on a stiff challenge. That was the kind of scene that has always tugged on my heart. Plus they were struggling uphill with snow flying in their faces, while I was hurrying downhill.

"Excuse me," an Asian-looking man asked, in barely audible English. "How far *MBC*?" My first thought from looking at this man was that he might have bitten off more than he could chew. *Don't lowball him.* I get sick of people doing that to me in foreign countries. On El Camino de Santiago, if you ask a Spaniard how far it is to a particular destination, you quickly learn to double, triple, if not quadruple the time given.

"One hour," I answered.

"One hour," he repeated in a disbelieving tone.

"Good luck," I said, and took off. The snow was now coming down in waves.

I finally saw a medium-sized group heading in the same direction as me. It was assuring to see I had company. But some selfish instincts also surfaced. I was banking on getting a room in *Deurali*; but this party of six would take up three rooms. *I have to get ahead of them.* Of course, the downhills were the place where my height actually helped me. Soon I passed by them.

As *Deurali* came into sight, the snow turned into a cold, pelting, possibly even dangerous, rain if a person couldn't get dry quickly. I poked my head into the first teahouse, where I was told they were full. With a sense of dread stirring, I did a beeline to the second one, and was relieved when a non-descript Nepali man calmly led me to a room. By the time I pulled every single item out of my backpack and put on several layers of clothing, heavy, slanting rain was sweeping across the area. *I'm very, very lucky to be here.*

***

I immediately pulled both beds together to lie down diagonally and then piled every single thing in the backpack on top of me. Soon I heard a knock. The same Nepali man was at the door.

"Other trekker need place to sleep. Can he stay in other bed?"

My mind immediately went back to when I had arrived at Thorung Phedi Base Camp, and the American man who had emphatically rejected the idea of anyone staying in his room. I had thought dimly of it at the time. However, I reasoned this was different because if an extra person stayed here, I would no longer be able to sleep diagonally. Instead, I would have to throw a single mattress on the cold floor. "No, I need both beds," I told the man. He walked away expressionless.

I was unable to get warm. After an hour in the bed, I walked into the dining room where I would spend the next four or five hours. A group of Russians, along with a lanky, middle-aged Frenchman (the man who had needed a bed) walked in together joking with each other. *Oh no, this could be unpleasant.*

But instead, what followed was an evening of the most pleasant surprises. For starters, the hosts brought some wood and poured it into a stove that lay under the table. Within 15 minutes, my lower body was toasty and upper body receiving encouraging vibes. The conversation with the other trekkers – nine males (8 Russians and one Frenchman) flowed as if among kindred souls.

The Frenchman, it ended up, was a mountain climber par excellence. "The first time I get to San Francisco," he recounted with gleeful wonder, "I ask, 'where the mountains'? I want to go to Yosemite'."

He had also done climbing in the Himalayas.

"How high have you been?" I asked.

"7,300 meters," he said. "I was going to 8,000 meters, but there were blizzards and my rope was swinging. I say to myself, 'Why go die'?" He was in his mid-fifties, but had a boyish enthusiasm about him that was infectious.

The Russians were – well, very Russian. But that ain't bad either, as I was to see. I was all about trying to stay warm. Of course, Russians are legendary in that regard. "The cold weather had a devastating effect on the German soldier," I remember reading in a history of the Second World War. "Even when it looked like they were winning in their invasion of Mother Russia, they were losing." These Russians had on jackets, but weren't all huddled up like most of us westerners. Truth be known, they looked more confident than any people I had been around in days.

"What do you think of Putin?" I couldn't resist asking. Don't worry – I wasn't looking to create an international incident.

"We need a strong leader." Time and again, they voiced a deeply-held desire for such a leader, which shouldn't be a surprise to anyone with a cursory knowledge of Russian history. Soon he launched into a tirade against Mikhail Gorbachev who, of course, we revere in the West (but is reviled in Russia).

"Ukraine, Byelorrusia, and Kazakhstan should be part of a

union with Russia," one of them firmly opined.

"You do not think those countries deserve their independence?" I asked.

"We are better together," he maintained. "The countries are too much alike."

I"ve learned over the years to give foreigners a wide berth in their opinions. Sometimes you can learn something when you least expect it.

"Has Putin made your lives better?"

"I'm here on Annapurna Circuit in Nepal," a quiet man on the far end of the table who could have passed for a thousand different Americans I have seen back home in the USA, answered solemnly. "In 2000 when he become President, I not be able to do Annapurna." Point well taken. In fact, it reminded of another conversation I had with a Ukrainian trekker recently about Mikhail Gorbachev.

"He won a Nobel Peace Prize," I said to her.

"Yes, but he bring hunger to the people."

Bring hunger to the people. The voice in which she had said it had been so pure I had felt gutted; it had overwhelmed any political debating point I might make. Rather, my predominant emotion had been *this woman knows what the hell she's talking about.* And even though I certainly disagreed with these guys about the desirability of Putin dominating their neighbors, they sounded like they knew very much what they were talking about as to why they able to do the Annapurna Circuit. More power to them.

For me, conversations like these are one of the major reasons to go abroad in the first place. And best of all, the conversation had piqued my interest enough to even get warm.

***

All smiles as we're headed down

"Good morning, Bill." It was the lilting English voice of Martha.

"How was *MBC* last night?"

"Bloody cold," she replied like she also knew what she was talking about. "I got out of there first thing."

I bid the Russians good luck and goodbye (although we would later have a reunion on the streets of Kathmandu) and set off for lower elevations and warmer climes with Martha. Along the way we ran into Dannika and Willums. While the Dutch and English were less likely to wear their worries on their sleeves than a lanky American, the entire atmosphere had palpably changed. We were getting ready to leave this land of cold, altitude, and rushing water behind. Everybody was secure and the mood was lighthearted.

"What was it like at ABC last night?" I asked.

"Very cold," Dannika immediately answered. "But very beautiful at sunrise."

About the time we got to *Dovan*, the skies opened up with torrents of rain. But not even that was cause for acute concern anymore. The four of us stopped to dine in a teahouse. A group of Canadians walked into the dining room, sporting the familiar grim looks of trekkers ascending in foul weather. They began intensively debriefing us about what lay ahead. Perhaps unsurprisingly, the report I rendered was a bit less encouraging than what my comrades reported to them.

My hope was to make it all the way down to Chomrong today; that was going to be a stretch. But the logic of lower altitude – and better and cheaper food – provided the impetus to make the necessary paces. By late afternoon, we were bounding up the stone steps into Chomrong, which we had left just over two days ago.

When Martha told me at dinner that she had another two weeks remaining in Nepal, that immediately set me off.

"Hey, you have time to do most of the Annapurna Circuit," I said.

"Is there any way to do just part of it?"

"Yes, you can now catch a ride part of the way up," I said.

"How much will it cost?"

"Well, these Nepali males look like hero-types. They might just have a female discount."

"Yes," she laughed knowingly. "A flutter of the eyelashes and turn of the heel, and perhaps the price will magically reduce."

I love turning people on to outdoor adventures – perhaps because I come from a country with an obesity rate of 30% nationwide. But also, I had first learned about the Annapurna Circuit, the Pacific Crest Trail, and El Camino de Santiago while on other treks. It's just the way outdoors people network. And almost invariably, these treks become a major part of a person's life.

That night Martha and I discussed her nascent journey on the Annapurna Circuit in detail. "Yes, I'm all in," she finally said, although I belatedly realized this had cost me a valued trekking partner for the rest of my descent. She diverted the very next day to the Circuit, and I was to miss her so very self-possessed style.

***

I left Chomrong alone the next day. The trail followed a series of painfully steep stone steps straight down the face of the mountain. But soon we were on a more normal trek, gliding along another rushing river.

That's when I ran into a large Chinese group, two members of whom I had superficially gotten to know on the ABC trek. Ironically, it was more difficult for the Chinese to make acquaintances amongst other trekkers than us westerners, despite the fact we were in a neighboring country much more similar to theirs. These two girls, *Ying* and *Tae,* acted like I was their best friend. Since I was always alert to the possibility of getting lost, I was glad to hang with their group as we went down, down, and more down.

However, my serenity received a jolt when we arrived at the bottom of yet another steep descent and found ourselves at a fork in the trail. One led pleasantly along the banks of the river. However, the other passed over the most rickety

Future Annapurna trekkers are not advised to follow my technique (or attitude!) crossing these suspensions

suspension bridge I have ever had the misfortune to peer upon. The Chinese group all pulled out their maps and began a discussion in Mandarin. *Please go straight.* I intently observed their discussion without understanding a word. But when they began pointing over the bridge, my stomach sank.

Ying and Tae started across, with their porters and guides in tow. Meanwhile, I began seriously considering just going straight and abandoning this group. *This trail going straight has to lead somewhere near where I'm trying to go.* But again, I lacked the courage of my convictions. And the minute I climbed onto the suspension bridge I realized it was worse than I had realized. The wooden boards on the bridge were far narrower and more flimsy than any I had yet crossed. The dozen or so members of the Chinese group all waited on the far side with their cameras out. Again, the most ghoulish thought occurred – *At least I'd have an audience…*

This bridge monopolized my attention in a way few things do. My mind rotated chaotically between feelings of helplessness, pulsations of naked fear, to outright anger at the trail designers. But I also received a trickle of encouragement with each step successfully taken. When I finally made it to the far side Ying and Tae hugged me, if in mocking fashion. So often it's the unexpected and unwanted that make a trip. "Will you send that photo to my e-mail address?" I asked her.

But then, to my confusion – to my utter confusion, in fact to my deep angst – the porters and guides began arguing among themselves and pointing back to the side we came from. The Chinese group had already set off along the eastern bank of the river when two of the porters went running after them.

"A problem?" I quickly asked one of the guides.

"The bridge. Wrong."

No.

Soon the group of Chinese reappeared, escorted by their two panting porters. Everybody was looking back at the other bank.

"We need to be on other side," Ying said.

"But we can take the path on this side and cross the river further down," I sharply rebutted (which may or may not have been true at all). Ying began closely examining her map.

"This is a nice path," I laid it on.

"No, this path go way up mountain," she replied (and would turn out to be correct).

"But this way will be pretty," I parried. "We will end up in the right place." Given the language barrier, I don't know if they picked up the desperation in my voice. In any event, my gambit did not succeed, as they all prepared to re-cross my least favorite bridge in the whole world. *I'm not going over that bridge ever again. It's ridiculous to do something that terrifies me so much.*

I began scanning my map closely. Yes, this path stayed along the banks of the river. But then it suddenly and sharply climbed a couple thousand feet. *This is the way you get in big trouble, by digging deeper. Who knows whether it is even well-maintained further down the river? Nope, you have to recross that bridge.*

I don't know if anybody has ever fallen over this suspension bridge. Maybe not. But I doubt anyone as tall as me has ever crossed it. My technique wasn't any more aesthetically pleasing the second time across, but I was able to relax my body weight more towards my lower body. Again I got a standing ovation upon my second traverse of this great body of water, which would be my last suspension bridge of any consequence in Nepal.

"We sorry," Ying said in a consoling voice.

"No problem," I replied. "I am glad to know Chinese make mistakes also."

CHAPTER 24

Himalayan Farewell

And that pretty much proved to be the end of my 'Himalayan crises'. For the most part, it was a cakewalk from here on out – and an enjoyable one at that. We began passing through more temperate climate zones, with the accompanying terraced fields and pastoral communities. Again, the fields were populated by people of widely varying ages. Seemingly everybody was carrying heavy loads of grass, fodder, wood, etc. They hardly looked up at us passing souls as they went about their labor.

Faces of authenticity and difficult to forget

Observing human variety can give pleasure. But sometimes, it's human sameness that is most enlightening. These fields full of human beings so hard at work might be classified as one of those Asian time warp scenes that travelers to these parts so frequently witness, a la *Norman Rockwell America*.

But I want to be careful to not over-glorify their circumstances. These here mortals do backbreaking work from practically the time they can walk, until they no longer are able to. Dilettantish westerners like to drop into Nepal and romanticize what is essentially a survivalist lifestyle. "There is poverty, but no misery," it is frequently said. And to be sure, we have a lot to learn from these denizens of one of the poorest countries in the world. But there is one salient point that is easily overlooked. We view going to a desperately poor country as an experience to be enjoyed and touted, before returning back home to our *bourgeouise* lifestyles in much more affluent countries, where we regale our friends about the wonders of these far-off lands. But these people hacking away in these fields – and not just them, but also all the street hawkers and hornblowers back in Kathmandu – they weren't going anywhere. This was it for them, and always had been from birth.

However, I do not think it would be overly romantic to say that while I was in Nepal for five weeks, at least a small part of Nepal would forever be in me. You simply can't have prolonged contact with such hardworking, yet material-deprived, people and not walk away with a profound respect for the virtues of a hands-on lifestyle, as well as an accompanying greater wariness of any and all sedentary avocations and passive wealth accumulation.

The next day I boarded another local bus, the likes of which I had hoped to never step foot on again. In fact, this one was more crowded by a factor of two or three, populated as it was with dogs and caged chickens. It was going straight to Pokhara, which lay at the foot of these mountains. The seats were jam-packed and out of the question; I stood clutching my backpack next to the so-called 'wingmen' on the steps leading into the bus, whose door was wide-open the whole way. This time the bus wound down a steep, winding road; we didn't actually get out of the mountains until entering the outskirts of Pokhara.

I bolted out of the bus at the very first stop in this teeming city, which is the second largest in Nepal. It was warm, the layout was flat, and I was hankering to walk. I had heard that the trekkers all stay down by the big lake. "Excuse me, lake?" I asked several people, Everybody knew the answer and helped rout me to that part of town. I passed by the local airport that takes the more extravagant trekkers back and forth to Kathamandu. Better yet, were the ethnic culinary delights that quickly caught the eye of somebody who has been in the mountains for 25 days. I popped into a Mediterranean restaurant and devoured a Kebob for a price of just over one dollar (100 rupees).

Finally, I arrived on the main street, running along Pokhara's big lake. It didn't take a real estate genius to come up with the idea of developing a major resort here. The lake, a crystal clear blue, was obviously a product of the runoff from the snow-capped mountains that hover so brilliantly over Pokhara. Trekkers, cars, and animals all coursed through the main street lined with trekker hotels. I had no idea where was the best place to stay and hardly even cared.

"Bill," I heard. It was Bar, along with a large group of Israelis, walking down the street licking ice-cream cones, which I savored at first sight.

"Where did you get that?" I asked, and quickly departed to make a purchase. Soon after, I ran into Ying and Tae.

"Bill, we stay in hotel just down the street," Ying said.

"Can you take me there?" I asked and followed them to a decent enough hotel, run and owned by Chinese, with nothing but Chinese trekkers, and now one American. I stayed there for three days. The first night I committed an atrocity at a local buffet with these two Chinese girls, and the next day we took a boat ride and climbed up a mountain to a Buddhist temple. The whole time in Pokhara I kept running into familiar Australian, French, British, Austrian, and even American trekkers, only their faces uniformly seemed much less taut than just several days before.

We had all lived quite a bit in those mountains towering above us. It felt good.

***

In closing this outdoor narrative, I am again overcome with gratefulness at my fortune to have been able to take such a great journey, to a wondrous country, and to have met so many inspiring people. The reason that last sentence is more truth than hyperbole has to do with its very nature – it was an outdoor journey on foot. That says a lot right there.

In fact, that has been one of the very few great discoveries of my adult life. Sorry for any presumptuousness, but anybody who has made it this far in the book is probably a kindred spirit. The way to travel is outdoors and on foot.

In my favorite poem, *Song of the Open Road*, Walt Whitman wrote:

O public road, I say back I am not afraid to leave you,
Yet I love you,
You express me better than I can express myself,

I think heroic deeds were all conceiv'd in the open air,
And all free poems also,
I think whatever I shall meet on the open road I shall like,
And whoever beholds me shall like me,
I think whoever I see must be happy.

BILL WALKER

Acknowledgments

When I got into long-distance hiking at age 44, I fell under the influence of an ultra-minimalist by the name of Warren Doyle. Warren has hiked the entire 2,181 mile Appalachian Trail sixteen times. His secret – besides his legendary stubbornness, is that he carries so little weight ("You don't need gloves. Just use a spare pair of socks.").

Considering myself an underdog to hike the entire trail, I was receptive to much of his message. For that reason I have never carried a heavy camera on my long-distance hikes. However, I greatly enjoy writing about these journeys. And while many photos might be overrated, that is not the case with the Himalayas.

Fortunately, a Scottish girl, Bronwen Sleigh, a Welsh printmaker living in Edinborough, Scotland stepped into the breach. Indeed, she showed an artist's touch in selecting several photos to send me. Thanks, Bronwen.

Also, as much as I freaked out, obsessed over, and whined about suspension bridges, it was only logical to have a photo of one in the book. Ying, an especially friendly trekker from Shanghai China, took a photo of me in a state of high anxiety as I crossed an especially flimsy suspension. Thanks Ying. And hopefully you will tell all your compatriots about the wonders of the Annapurna region. Like the Europeans, the Americans, and the Nepalis, the more Chinese trekkers, the better.

Finally, on the bus returning to Kathamandu, I met Kara Parker, a recent graduate of the University of Washington and a member of its downhill ski team. Kara is probably a good example of the newly liberated female traveler. She and her friend seemingly covered the entire Eastern Hemisphere in their post-university trek. I urge those of you contemplating such an open-ended adventure to check out her website at *www.kjparker17.wixcom/thekaravan#* And, of course, I want to thank her for the photo she donated to me of herself and her friend 'getting high'.

About the Author

Bill Walker was born and raised in Macon, Georgia. He received a Bachelor's and Master's Degree in Accounting from the University of Georgia. From 1985-1999, he was a commodities broker at the Chicago Board of Trade and London International Financial Futures Exchange. Later he taught English as a Second Language in five Latin American countries.

His first book, *Skywalker – Close Encounters on the Appalachian Trail*, was a narrative of his 2005 thru-hike of the Appalachian Trail. His second book, *Skywalker – Highs and Lows on the Pacific Crest Trail*, told the story of his hike of the 2,663 mile Pacific Crest Trail, in which he lost 43 pounds. Walker has also walked The Camino de Santiago pilgrimage in France and Spain for the last three years. His narrative, *The Best Way – El Camino de Santiago*, covers the first two of those pilgrimages.

Walker, who is just shy of 7-feet tall, is currently working on a whimsical book on the subject of height. He lives in Asheville, North Carolina.

Message From the Author

I would like to express my sincere gratitude for you choosing this narrative. The fondest hope of any author is to inspire readers to undertake some theretofore unknown pursuit. Indeed, the Annapurna Circuit lived up to its reputation as the best way for an average person such as myself to directly experience the world's greatest mountain range, the Himalayas. Those of you who are interested have a thrilling new chapter ahead in your lives.

Finally, if you see fit, a written review on Amazon would be greatly appreciated (three or four lines is plenty). These reviews are tremendously helpful to us independent authors.

Thank you and *Namaste,*

Bill Walker, March 5, 2013

Made in the USA
Middletown, DE
20 January 2018